D1634044

JUMBO

By the same author

Marconi (1972)
Sir Oliver Lodge (1974)
Lord Leverhulme (1976)

Why part with Jumbo (The Pet of the Zoo)?

W. P. JOLLY

CONSTABLE LONDON

First published in Great Britain 1976
by Constable and Company Ltd
10 Orange Street London WC2H 7EG

ISBN 0 09 461340 0

Filmset in Monophoto Garamond and
printed in Great Britain by
BAS Printers Limited, Wallop, Hampshire

Contents

Credits for illustrations

Zoological Society of London: 14, 25, 30, 36, 65, 87, 89, 109, 112, 113, 119, 120, 149, 155
Mary Evans Picture Library: 12, 40, 42, 44, 51, 53–58, 69, 72, 92, 97, 98, 100, 102, 105, 127, 158
Ascherberg, Hopwood & Crew: 21
Radio Times Hulton Picture Library: 48
City Museum & Art Gallery, Hanley, Stoke-on-Trent: 131
National Maritime Museum: 106
Harvard Theatre Collection: 134, 143
American Museum of Natural History: 157
British Museum, Natural History: 159, 160
National Film Archive: 163
Tufts University: 156

Introduction

A biographer takes an elephant as his subject with some misgiving, but at least he has no worry about offending the family, nor is he overburdened with personal papers. In writing the story of Jumbo there was, however, an unexpected and recurrent bonus. Librarians and archivists, busy with profound and scholarly enquiries, seemed to unbend at the mention of Jumbo's name, and the excellent service they always give was in this case seasoned with a smile. But, even if they enjoyed the work, I thank them for their help.

I must particularly acknowledge the paramount contribution to the book by Maureen Jolly and Mostyn Gilbert who did so much of the research in Britain and the United States. Personal thanks are also due to Joan Crammond, Anne Jolly, John King, and Barbara Morris.

Of the many institutions whose staffs have helped me, I am specially indebted to the British Library at Bloomsbury and Colindale, the British Museum (Natural History), the Victoria and Albert Museum, the London Library, the Mary Evans Picture Library, the Beaverbrook Newspapers Library, the National Maritime Museum, the Zoological Society of London, the American Museum of Natural History New York, Harvard University, and Tufts University.

The sources of quotations, etc., are given in Notes (page 167) and copyright material is used with the gracious permission of Her Majesty The Queen, and of the Council of the Zoological Society of London, the Director of the City Museum and Art Gallery, Hanley, and the National Film Archive.

WPJ. April 1976

The Noah's Ark Society

Jumbo the elephant was the most famous animal in the world, and millions of words were written about him in the British and American Press. When Barnum bought him from the London Zoo and shipped him to the United States in 1882 there was an extraordinary outburst of 'Jumbomania'. Special editions of newspapers were brought out, Jumbo songs were performed in the music-halls, Jumbo souvenirs were turned out in thousands, and crowds of Jumbo's fans gathered noisily in the streets of London and New York.

Museums on both sides of the Atlantic still display relics of Jumbo, but his chief memorial is his name in the language: the child's affectionate term for an elephant, and the commercial jargon for anything where size is made a virtue.

The elephant's size alone accounts for much of the fascination which the animal has always exerted over the human race. His shape is ridiculous: a huge blob with a little post at each corner and punctuated by an absurdly small eye with chorus-girl lashes. As if this were not enough of a joke there is a tail at each end: the one too small and the other too big. As Hilaire Belloc wrote,

When people call this beast to mind,
They marvel more and more
At such a LITTLE tail behind,
So LARGE a trunk before.

But the amusement provoked by his appearance is affectionate not derisive, and the smiles are tinged with the awe and respect which caused oriental races to place the elephant among the gods. People find the mysterious, powerful mountain of flesh particularly attractive because it shares many human characteristics. The elephant lives about three score years and ten, its social life is highly developed, and the young do not become independent until they reach their teens. A family group may consist of a mother with a baby and an older offspring, an 'auntie' helping to look after the baby, and, some distance away, the father, huge and majestic. Several such groups, related to each other, make up the herd, which will probably be bossed, not by one of the magnificent bulls, but by an old cow—a matriarchal system not unknown to modern man.

The elephant's intelligence and memory are legendary and—unique among quadrupeds—it possesses a 'hand' (the old and rather better name for the trunk) with which it conveys food and drink to its mouth, and which is sufficiently sensitive, strong and adaptable to allow the animal to carry out all sorts of tasks and tricks. The trained elephant can stack tree trunks, wield a broom, uncork and swig the contents of a bottle, pick a button off a shelf fifteen feet high, or accept a sixpenny tip and slip it into its keeper's pocket.

Man's earliest interest in the elephant is evident in drawings and carvings preserved from prehistory, while the art and literature of China, India, Greece and Rome are rich in descriptions of the part played by the great beasts in human affairs during the last few centuries B.C. The elephant with a wooden 'castle' on his back containing half a dozen bowmen or other soldiers was a terror weapon often deployed on the battlefield. The elephant and castle were common enough as an English inn sign and if, as some said, this was a corruption of 'Infanta of Castile', then Dickens recorded a case of corruption corrupted, with an 'Elephant and Castle' in Liverpool which by 1851 had become known as the 'Pig and Whistle'.[1]

Roman generals included their military elephants in triumphal parades, and preserved those captured from the enemy for slaughter in recherché ways to make a spectacle for the mob. But the modern history of the exhibition of the elephant in Europe for the interest and entertainment of a relatively civilized public can probably be reasonably considered to date from the thirteenth century.

In A.D. 1255 the King of France presented Henry III of England with an elephant which was shipped across the Channel to London where Henry ordered the Sheriff to 'cause without delay, to be built at our Tower of London one house of forty feet long and twenty feet deep, for our elephant'.[2] Another, later, bout of royal 'pass the elephant' brought one to Elizabeth I—a present this time from Henry IV of France. The royal menagerie at the Tower was maintained for nearly six centuries, and when it closed, the animals, including an elephant, were moved to Regent's Park to augment the very modest collection of the Zoological Society of London, or Noah's Ark Society, newly founded in 1826 by Sir Stamford Raffles. During the second half of the seventeenth century there was in the menagerie at Versailles an elephant who excited the admiration of the French by drinking a dozen bottles of wine daily, and during the first half of the eighteenth century there were elephants on display in Paris at the Jardin des Plantes, botanical gardens established in 1626 to which an animal collection was later added. The first elephant seen in the United States was imported from India in 1796 by a merchant sea captain and displayed widely throughout the country in circuses.

With the nineteenth century came increased exploration of tropical countries, improved sea and land transport, and the appearance of professional animal dealers who were prepared to supply live specimens to Europe and America to satisfy the new public interest in exotic creatures. It was the early 1800s which saw the great growth of menageries and circuses as popular entertainment.

In 1810 the largest elephant seen in England was secured by the manager of the Covent Garden Theatre for nine hundred guineas.[3] The animal made his debut in a new pantomime, *Harlequin Padmenaba*, and was extremely popular with audiences. But no matter how much of a crowd-puller he may be, an elephant on the stage poses problems. The difficulties and embarrassments which attend a theatrical performance by any animal are all present, but on a gigantic scale. To maintain an elephant as an occasionally used 'prop' is unacceptably troublesome and expensive, while to regard him as an ordinary actor performing week by week in different plays would necessarily endow the company's repertoire over the years with a certain bizarre singularity which could easily become wearisome. The Covent Garden Theatre soon let its elephant go: down the road to a permanent indoor menagerie in Exeter 'Change, just off the Strand, whose manager had coveted the beast ever since it had first been shown in England.

The same year as the Covent Garden management first coaxed their big star onto the stage in pantomime, the Duke of Devonshire set up—albeit involuntarily—what might be considered to have been the forerunner of the aristocratic safari parks. At a party to bid *bon voyage* to a

Baby Jumbo in 1865

friend about to sail for India, the Duke had jokingly said that he would love to own an elephant. Many months later a huge horse-drawn van appeared unexpectedly at the Duke's country house in Chiswick and from it was led an elephant, a gift from the friend in India. But the Duke and his staff were as unruffled by the new arrival as they would have been to receive an eccentric relative or a capricious guest. The elephant was provided with suitable quarters, enquiries were made about her diet, and with the head gardener allocated as her keeper, she remained at Chiswick for many years, learning like any sophisticated house-party *habituée* to perform little tricks and services for the entertainment and gratification of the family and their friends.

A few doors away from the menagerie in Exeter Street, off the Strand, was the 'tonsorial establishment' of Mr Turner, the father of the artist. Mr Turner was a hairdresser and brushmaker, and one of his senior employees was a man called Bartlett, who had a son, Abraham Dee Bartlett, born in 1812.[4] Young Bartlett was allowed to wander freely in and out of the neighbouring menagerie, and when he was just a toddler he used to play with lion cubs and other animals which were judged unlikely to harm him. As quite a young boy he began to experiment with the bodies of small animals which had died in the menagerie, removing and preparing their skins for stuffing. By the time he was thirteen or fourteen he was a competent taxidermist, but it never occurred to anyone that this interest might provide him with a career, and he was apprenticed to his father, doing work which he hated, although some might have thought that there was at least a certain small affinity between dressing the hair of the living and the fur of the dead. He continued with his taxidermy as a hobby and by good fortune obtained, through a customer of the hairdressing salon, introductions to the Zoological Society and to the British Museum. He gradually built up a profitable connection as a freelance taxidermist, and in 1851 he won a prize at the Great Exhibition, for a display of stuffed animals, and this led to him finally escaping from

the tonsorial trade. He was offered and accepted the post of naturalist to the Crystal Palace Company when Paxton's great greenhouse was moved from Hyde Park to its permanent site in the London suburb of Sydenham. Among the exhibits in his charge were large groups of stuffed animals and birds, arranged naturally among real shrubs and trees. The excellent sub-tropical growing conditions inspired the gardeners, who went enthusiastically about their work. But Bartlett could never persuade them that the water they sprayed so copiously on their plants was deadly to lions, serpents, even ducks, if stuffed. The plants flourished and the animals rotted. But Bartlett was soon able to move away from this unusual and unhappy situation and pursue his career as a naturalist among the living creatures in the Zoological Gardens where he was appointed Superintendent in 1859.

In 1865 Bartlett arranged an exchange of animals with the Jardin des Plantes. The Paris Zoo received a rhinoceros and in return sent to London a small African elephant. The French officials would have been very chastened if they had realised that they were providing the London Zoo with an exhibit which would generate profit and publicity far in excess even of the *succès fou* some years before when the Jardin des Plantes had acquired a giraffe which, a contemporary account recorded,[5] 'for several months occupied almost the exclusive attention of the lively Parisians. Every fashion was *à la giraffe*; and even the ladies wore dresses, and the men carried handkerchiefs, bearing the portrait of the animal.'

Opposite: *A. D. Bartlett*

The little elephant was the first one that had come under Bartlett's own immediate charge, and it was the London Zoo's first African elephant. He was called Jumbo.

Scott and little Jumbo

There is no record of when he received the name, but it was probably given to him by Bartlett. The word *jumbo* itself has African origins: a Zulu word *jumba* means a large packet, and since the eighteenth century *Mumbo Jumbo* had been applied in English to a powerful supernatural being from Africa. Many years later Bartlett gave the name Mumbo to a gorilla at the Zoo. There is a dictionary reference[6] as early as 1823 to *jumbo* meaning a clumsy or unwieldy fellow. But it was the little elephant who by the 1880s had made it a commonplace word to be found in the smallest dictionary.

When Jumbo arrived in London on 26 June 1865 he was just over five feet high and was judged to be about four years old.[7] Bartlett had formed his own firm ideas about the way in which elephants should be managed, and he intended to put these ideas into practice in bringing up the Zoo's new acquisition, who was little more than a baby. Bartlett wrote,[8] 'I handed him over to Matthew Scott, who I thought was the most likely man to attend to my instructions because he had no previous experience in the treatment and management of elephants.' Scott had been a keeper of antelopes, but he established an immediate *rapport* with Jumbo, and as the animal grew in size and fame so too did Scott's self-esteem. Eventually his autocratic attitude in all matters relating to his charge must often have caused the Superintendent to wish that he had selected someone else as keeper of the African elephant.

The long journey from the African interior, and the brief stay in Paris, had been almost too much for so young an elephant. His general condition was very poor when he arrived at Regent's Park. His skin was ingrained with filth, and his feet had grown badly out of shape because nails and hard callouses had not been attended to. Bartlett and Scott spent many hours with him, and under the Superintendent's instructions the keeper scrubbed and washed the animal, filed and pared his misshapen feet, and gave him carefully planned nourishing meals to build up his strength.

As he grew used to his new surroundings and his condition improved Jumbo, like a convalescent child in hospital, began to play up occasionally; to be disobedient, frolicsome and rough. Bartlett wrote, 'we found it necessary to put a stop to his gambols, and this we accomplished in a very speedy and effectual manner. Scott and myself, holding him by each ear, administered to him a good thrashing. He quickly recognised that he was mastered, by lying down and uttering a cry of submission.' Bartlett classed such treatment as 'necessary cruelty', which he distinguished from the unnecessary cruelty of the ignorant and the sadistic. He believed that in the management of an elephant 'unless the person in charge of him is determined to be master and overpower him, that person will lose all control over him and will be liable at any moment to fall victim to his enormous strength'. This was no groundless theory put forward by an insensitive man without experience of elephants. Bartlett had since childhood taken an intense interest in animals, he knew most of the menagerie owners and animal dealers, and in the particular case of the elephant he was well aware of the difficulties and dangers that could arise with such a huge beast in close confinement.

Terrifying destruction can occur in the often considerable time it may take to subdue an elephant who gets out of control. In 1848 an elephant named Rayah killed his keeper and, since he had previously killed another man, it was decided that he should be put down.[9] He was given a bun containing enough poison to kill several thousand men, but appeared to relish it, and when thirty soldiers of a rifle company were called in to do the job it took two volleys, each of fifteen shots, to kill him. Bartlett himself, as a boy of fourteen, had personally witnessed the chaotic scenes at the Exeter Street menagerie when Chunee, once the star at Covent Garden Theatre, ran amok and was killed.[10] Everyone was astonished and frightened at the fury of the charges made again and again by the maddened elephant. Poison had no effect and there was a very real danger that the beast might break out of his enclosure and bring the whole building down in ruins. Eventually a detachment of Foot Guards was rushed up from the nearby barracks, but even then shot after shot had to be fired into the wretched animal, and only after he had been hit 152 times was he pronounced dead. The noisy, bloody affair made a great impression upon young Bartlett, and he determined that any elephant under his charge should be strictly controlled so that there would be no repetition at the Zoo of the horrifying and dangerous killing of poor Chunee.

But if Bartlett believed in stern control he also believed in kindness. After little Jumbo's disciplinary beating, as soon as he had shown submission Bartlett and Scott made a fuss of him and fed him titbits, and, Bartlett wrote, 'after this time he appeared to recognize that we were his best friends'.

A few months after Jumbo came to the Zoo, Bartlett bought a second African elephant. The transaction is recorded in the Zoological Gardens Day Book[11] for Saturday, 9 September 1865: '1 African Elephant ♀ £550 including 1 Hornbill, 1 Crow, 1 Guineafowl, 6 Finches from Mr Rice.' The Superintendent himself collected his elephant, a female, and walked her to Regent's Park accompanied by over a hundred of the mob of ragged boys and idle men who were always available in the streets of Victorian London to lend their support to any free spectacle.

At the Zoo the new arrival was given the name Alice and housed next door to Jumbo.

The Press—always ready to put one and one together with public figures, even if they were elephants—soon linked the names of Jumbo and Alice, and steadfastly cultivated the illusion of a romantic attachment when in fact the two animals hardly ever met and were not even good friends.

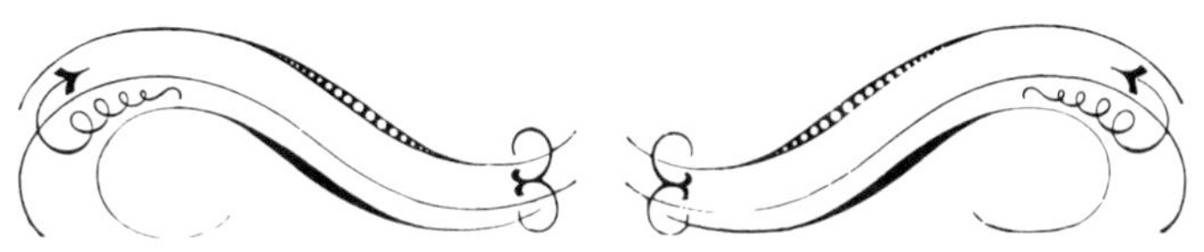

Walking in the Zoo

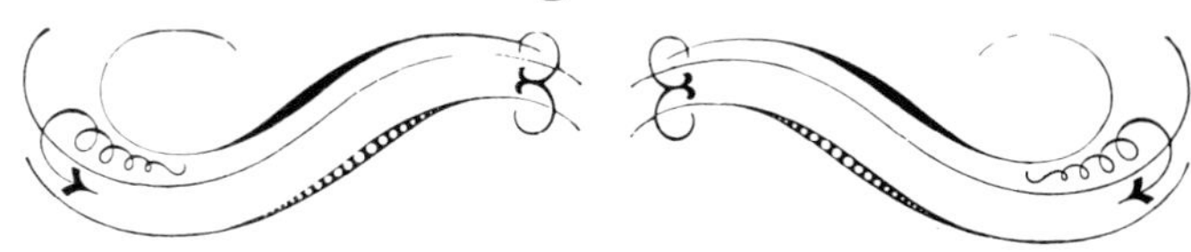

The Stilton, Sir, the Cheese, the O.K. thing to do
On Sunday afternoon is to toddle in the Zoo.
Weekdays may do for cads, but not for me or you,
So dressed right, down the street, we show them who is
who.

The walking in the Zoo, walking in the Zoo,
The O.K. thing on Sundays is the walking in the Zoo.[1]

In 1867 George Vance—The Great Vance of Victorian music-hall posters—strutted and posed on the stage as an extravagantly immaculate swell, and in exaggerated stage-posh style half sang and half recited these words, reflecting the great attraction of the Zoo at this time for the general public as well as for the fashionable set. Vance was one of that specialized and popular group of Victorian entertainers—including some women—who dressed themselves as dandies, and sang songs which reassured bibulous audiences in the gilt and plush of Palace and Metropolitan that the 'toffs' in the harsh world outside were aimless, brainless, and possibly shirtless too, and were to be laughed at rather than envied or feared.

The Fellows of the London Zoological Society looked with disfavour upon this new word 'Zoo', which they regarded as a vulgar diminutive of the accepted name, Zoological Gardens. But vulgar words, like weeds, often flourish unwanted, and the novel term introduced by

Vance took root firmly in London, and then spread rapidly over Britain and the rest of the world until, today, there are few countries where it is not common or at least recognised.

Walking in the Zoo on Sundays was a privilege reserved for Fellows and their friends. It was important to refer to 'a walk in the Zoo' like a walk in the Park. A visit to the Zoo sounded too much like a visit to a place of entertainment, which would have been out of the question on the Sabbath.

The Zoo had first been opened to the general public in 1847, with an admission charge of a shilling, and as the collection of animals grew, and better transport facilities were provided between central London and Regent's Park, public support increased rapidly. Between about 1860 and 1890 was a boom time for the Zoo, a time of great improvement in its financial and scientific standing which began at roughly the same time as Bartlett became Superintendent and Thomas Huxley succeeded the Prince Consort as President.

There was a succession of sharp peaks in this growing public interest, each produced by the arrival at the Zoo of some animal which particularly caught the popular imagination and became a star attraction. Tommy the chimpanzee came to London, travelling with his keeper by stage-coach from the Bristol docks. Obaysch the hippopotamus was presented to Queen Victoria by the Viceroy of Egypt in 1850, and he was the first of his kind to be seen in Europe for many years. The baby hippo arrived in the Zoological Gardens with a retinue appropriate to his royal connection: an Arab attendant who remained for a year to see him settled in, and a small flock of sheep and goats who had provided milk on the long journey from the Nile. Jim the Indian rhinoceros was a marvel of powerful ugliness and frightening ill-temper which fascinated the Victorian crowds. The long roll of Zoo favourites and money-spinners winds steadily on, with Brumas the polar bear cub of a generation ago and the giant pandas, which were yesteryear's politician's prize from China.

Walking in the Zoo

As he grew older and bigger, Jumbo quickly established a place for himself among the Zoo favourites, and was trained to carry a wooden structure on his back. It was nothing so glamorous as a silk-draped howdah, just two

WALKING IN THE ZOO
SUNG WITH DISTINGUISHED APPLAUSE BY
THE GREAT VANCE.
"WALKING IN THE ZOO, WALKING IN THE ZOO
THE O.K. THING ON SUNDAY IS THE WALKING IN THE ZOO,
WALKING IN THE ZOO, WALKING IN THE ZOO
THE O.K. THING ON SUNDAY IS THE WALKING IN THE ZOO."
WRITTEN BY
HUGH WILLOUGHBY SWENY ESQ
MUSIC BY
ALFRED LEE.

simple wood-backed benches, one slung high up on each side, on which the passengers sat sideways with their backs to the elephant and their knees facing outward. Half a dozen or more passengers could be carried at a time, with the keeper leading the elephant along paths in the Gardens thronged with people who sometimes pressed rather too close for safety. The cargo almost invariably consisted of half-scared, half-grinning children, although occasionally some privileged or potentially generous man might be permitted to sit precariously astride the huge back, but there was no way in which a lady could have enjoyed the treat without a quite unimaginable public loss of decorum.

Jumbo was not the first of the Zoo's riding elephants. For many years this had been one of the attractions at Regent's Park, built up into a coveted treat for children by the elephant keepers, some of whom thereby gratified a certain taste for theatrical exhibitionism, and all of whom profited considerably from the fact that there was no official charge for a ride, the custodian of the elephant being allowed to keep any tips offered of their own free will by the custodians of the young passengers. It was a rewarding game to be in charge of a riding elephant on a busy summer day, chaffing and encouraging the lucky children on his back and warning the less fortunate mere spectators to stand well clear of the swinging trunk which 'could knock yer 'ead off'.

All the riding elephants before Jumbo had been of the Indian variety—indeed Jumbo was the Zoo's first African elephant. Even to the layman's eye there are noticeable differences between the two species, and to the zoologist the external and internal differences are sufficient for the Indian animal to be placed in the genus *Elephas* and the African in *Loxodonta*. Thus these two surviving members of the order *Proboscidea*, which included the mammoths and many other strange prehistoric animals, are known as *Elephas maximus* and *Loxodonta africana*.[2]

The African elephant is generally larger. Typically, a fully grown African bull might be eleven feet tall, weigh seven tons, and have tusks seven feet long. The Indian bull would be over a foot shorter, weigh six tons, and have tusks less than five feet long. The females are smaller, with roughly proportional differences between the two species, except that the Indian female's tusks are insignificant or non-existent, while the African female's are quite long. The trunk of the African elephant has two 'fingers' at the end where the Indian has only one. But most distinctive of all are the very large ears of African elephants, shaped rather like the map of Africa, while the smaller ears of the Indian elephant are reminiscent of the Indian sub-continent.

It was widely believed in the 1800s that the African elephant could not be tamed and would not live in captivity, a view which was supported by the absence in the nineteenth century of any domesticated African elephants, in contrast with a long history of service to man by the Indian species. Nevertheless many of the Roman and Carthaginian military elephants had been African, and the London Zoo had Jumbo—and indeed Alice—as evidence of successful management. Bartlett was however quite clear that the African and Indian species were distinguished as much by temperament as by physical differences. He wrote[3] that his experience led him to believe that African elephants required 'a much greater amount of skill and attention than the more docile Indian species. The male African elephant we have in the Gardens, I believe, is the largest living example in Europe. He is amazingly intelligent, good-tempered, and tractable; at the same time he has given me, and every one who has had anything to do with him, constant and increasing trouble and anxiety. First his enormous strength and restless disposition, together with his determined desire to be at large, have kept us day after day constantly employed altering, repairing, and making his house strong enough to keep him in it.'

Bartlett believed that in spite of such difficulties the African elephant might be trained to be a valuable source of powerful labour in his own continent (a Belgian experiment in the Congo in the 1900s later supported this view) but he felt that the ultimate fate of the animal was probably already determined by the long-established African policy of using men, often slaves, as beasts of burden, and of killing elephants in their tens of thousands for the lucrative ivory trade.

From man's earliest history he had sought ivory because it could easily be made into tools and weapons which were both sharp and strong. When painters, jewellers, sculptors, and even architects, adopted the material almost universally as an artistic medium, the hunting of elephants for their tusks became highly organised. The hunt became a slaughter with the relatively modern popularisation of the piano, billiards, and ivory-handled cutlery, and with the more or less simultaneous availability of fire-arms. An estimate of the annual consumption of ivory by England alone in Bartlett's time was 1,200,000 pounds, corresponding to some 30,000 elephants, mostly African because they produced more easily workable ivory. Bartlett feared that the African elephant might not survive long into the twentieth century. The fact that its extinction has been avoided, though only just, may be attributed to the synthetic materials of the organic chemists on the one hand, and to the legislation of the conservators on the other, although the struggle is not yet over and only recently an African country has felt it necessary to invoke the death penalty for ivory poaching. Meanwhile in Asia modern technology provides the bulldozer and similar vehicles to take over more and more of the work of the highly domesticated and more docile Indian elephant. Not that the Indian elephant was unfailingly tractable. The special pension rates payable to the widows of mahouts testify to the docile beasts' occasional outbursts, and even under Bartlett's careful management at the Zoological Gardens, Jack the Indian elephant, with a combination of cunning and strength, managed to get hold of a rhinoceros who lived in the next compound and, by holding him with his tusks against the bars separating their enclosures, broke his neighbour's ribs and crushed the life out of him.

Conditions at the Zoo, although cramped compared with natural life in the wild, were in general very favourable to the physical well-being of the inmates. Certainly this was the case with the elephants, who thrived to the extent that visitors from countries where these beasts roamed wild commented on the health and size of those in the Gardens. At Regent's Park there was always warm, dry shelter for the elephants, they were less likely to suffer injury than animals pushing their way through bush or jungle, and constant attention, bathing, and grooming

A ride on Jumbo

kept them free of parasites and superficial infections that might have caused debilitating illness. Above all they had a generous, carefully planned diet of hay, boiled rice, bread, and greenstuff, supplemented by very large quantities of buns, rolls, biscuits and fruit supplied by visitors who were endlessly delighted to feel a titbit snuffled out of their palm by the questing trunk and then curled casually back into the tiny mouth with a brief acknowledging flap of the huge ears that looked like old grey canvas. The public's whim was profitably indulged by the Zoo authorities who allowed a woman to sell rolls, cake, and fruit[4] 'for the use of the elephant alone under the direction of the keeper in charge of the animal'. This was on the whole a more satisfactory arrangement than an alternative when, at one time, the refreshment room sold its stale cakes for the same purpose, leaving an uneasy doubt in the public mind about the precise age at which a bun passed on from the human to the elephant menu.

Jumbo certainly thrived on the diet and grew to the point where he could only just get through the tunnel, something over eleven feet high, which joined two sections of the Zoological Gardens. He was undoubtedly a magnificent animal, to the credit and satisfaction of Bartlett and Scott, the two dissimilar men most concerned with his upbringing.

Bartlett was very much the Superintendent, with white hair and long white beard. He usually wore a top hat and frock-coat when he went about the Zoo, but this in no way inhibited him from undertaking menial tasks, or even dangerous ones, if he felt that example or emergency required it. He was a sympathetic, thoughtful man with an enquiring scientific mind which was not however without its prejudices and irrational touches of mysticism. He published over fifty serious papers in the Proceedings of the Zoological Society and yet at the same time he was intellectually mesmerised by the number seven, looking everywhere for examples of its special significance—perhaps he would have found the binary 111 even more mystic than the decimal 7.

In some ways his role in the world of Zoological Gardens was not unlike that of Dr Arnold of Rugby in the world of the public school. He had enlightened but unsentimental ideas about the discipline and training of the creatures given into his charge, some of them fit to mix in the most polite circles, some whose amusing antics might too often end in embarrassing scenes, and some so savage, unpredictable, or poisonous as to be quite unfit for human society. In other ways Bartlett was perhaps more like Dr Barnardo, accepting into his establishment all sorts of miserable, unwanted waifs, and noting and measuring their emaciated and sickly condition before building them up for public display.

Bartlett would risk his life to extract a huge decayed tooth for a hippopotamus; would experiment and search tirelessly to find the best diet for a baby monkey; would dissect a dead elephant, by the side of the road surrounded by hundreds of spectators, to try to discover the cause of death; would seek out and confront a known pickpocket reported in the Zoological Gardens; and faced with another dead elephant he extracted the brain for the Royal College of Surgeons and then struck a bargain with a passing catsmeat man, who paid a sovereign for the right to remove the mountain of flesh and then found himself with one of the more memorable bad bargains when the pampered pussies of London NW turned up their noses at the unusual flavour and texture.

Though London cats might occasionally eat elephant, the cats of Paris appeared on their owners' menus during the siege of 1871, and Jumbo himself was lucky to have come to London a few years before from the Jardin des Plantes where most of the animals were eaten by the starving Parisians.

Jumbo's keeper, Matthew Scott, was a rougher but not a tougher man than Superintendent Bartlett. He was sturdy, strong and self-assured in the manner of the successful Victorian working man. He had a fine moustache and usually wore a pepper and salt suit and a curly bowler. There was the hint of a swagger about him as he left the Gardens for a midday drink at a handy public-house much favoured by the keepers. Scott's position in the unofficial hierarchy of keepers improved as Jumbo became not only the largest but also the most popular of all the animals.

The Spectator wrote,[5] 'as to the elephants, they are all friends of the public, if only because they can be fed, and among them "Jumbo" in particular is *the* friend, for a very natural reason. He alone realises the popular ideal. It is not to be denied that interesting as every elephant is and must be—being the only beast whose nose is as long as an arm, and as efficient as a hand—most elephants, and especially most Indian elephants, disappoint the public as much as the Atlantic Ocean is said to have disappointed Mr Oscar Wilde. There is so little of them. The public, deceived partly by pictures, and partly by the very remarkable disparities existing among elephants, expects a mountain of flesh, and on seeing an animal only half as large again as a bull, feels as deceived as when it goes to see a giant, and finds only a meek and weak-kneed life-guardsman, and almost asks for its money back. It regards the elephants as *the* sight of the Zoological, and wants its children to be not only amazed, but a little alarmed. "It 'ud weigh," remarked a meditative butcher of one Indian beast, "but 'taint so big as I thought." "Jumbo" is as big. Belonging to the big African species, and probably sprung from an aristocratic family with a tendency to body, caught young, and therefore sufficiently fed—a wild elephant rarely gets quite enough to eat—he has developed in his early adolescence into an amazing, almost portentous, beast. There is no elephant like him in Europe, and, we imagine, very few indeed like him anywhere, certainly not in the greatest collections in the world—the elephant Kheddahs maintained by the Government of India. He is, though probably not quite full grown, nearly twelve feet high, a height our readers will realise if they glance up to their own ceiling, and reflect where the back of the elephant would be, and remember how big a dray-horse twice his usual height would look.

Outside his den, "Jumbo" gives the impression of a moving mountain, makes raw spectators gape with content and a sense of gratified ideals, and inspires in children a feeling that to mount him is a feat of heroism to be recounted even in after-life. They are delighted with him after they get down, for they feel they have done something brave and risky, and if they had ever seen "Jumbo" in the tunnel with a loaded waggon passing overhead, they would be confirmed in that impression. Unless they take to whaling, he is the biggest living thing they are ever likely to touch or see . . . .'

Jumbo was at the height of his popularity, if not his fame, but a time was approaching when he would have much more to upset his equanimity than the occasional sound of a waggon passing overhead in the tunnel, and when that time came no one but Bartlett or Scott would dare touch him.

A dignified load (Bartlett aloft in top hat, Scott holding Jumbo's trunk)

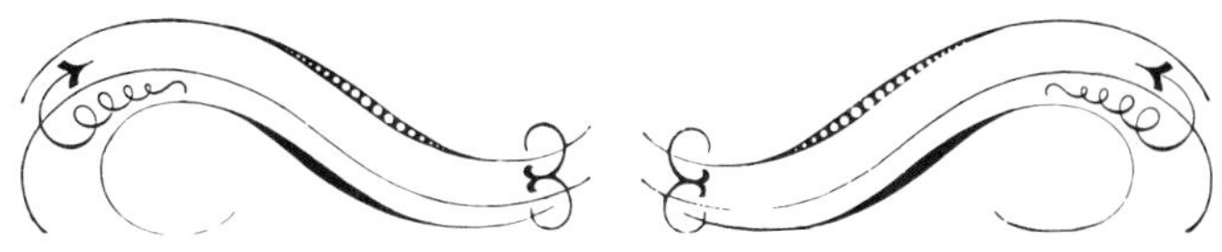

Trouble with pachyderms

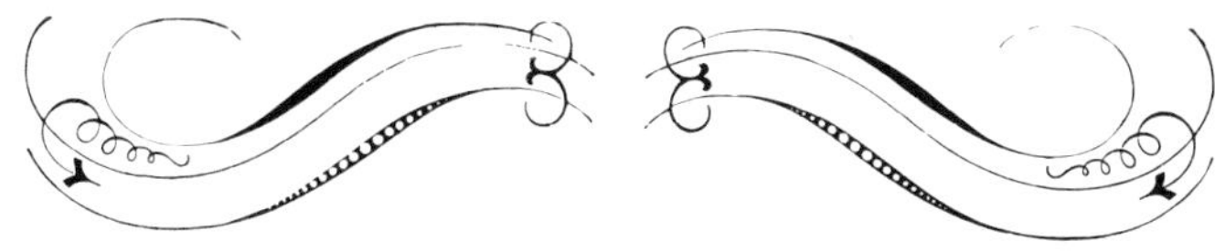

For nearly fifteen years after he arrived at the London Zoo Jumbo gave very little trouble, made the turnstiles click profitably, and was a source of tremendous pleasure to many thousands of visitors of all ages and all stations, including Queen Victoria herself and the children of the Royal Household. Other elephants occasionally caused alarms and commotions: Alice tore nearly twelve inches off the end of her trunk, but Bartlett and the keepers put food and drink by hand into her mouth until the wound healed and she was able to use her trunk almost as well as before; an Indian elephant hemmed in by crowds in the Broad Walk accidentally knocked over his keeper, crushing the man's thigh so badly that he died after an operation to amputate the leg. But such incidents were rare with the elephants. Of the larger animals, it was the untamed rhinos and hippos who most often figured in the Zoo's dramas, and in the comedies that would have been an inspiration to Mack Sennet and the Keystone Cops.

In 1865 two young rhinos were to be moved from their house to winter quarters a hundred yards or so away in the Gardens. Bartlett decided to carry out the operation at first light, and so, early one morning, he and all the keepers gathered outside the rhinoceros enclosure. First of all a strong collar was slipped over the head of each rhino, then each beast had two long stout ropes attached to its collar and half a dozen men were assigned to catch hold of each rope to restrain and guide the animal on its brief journey through the Gardens. The collars and ropes were safely fitted and the two dozen keepers assembled outside the enclosure waiting to take up their restraining positions on the ropes. The gates were opened and a keeper with a bundle of fresh hay attracted the animals' attention and walked in front of them, leading them out of the enclosure. This stage went as planned and the two animals came out into the roadway following the keeper with the hay at a gentle pace. But as soon as they saw the waiting crowd of men who pressed forward to take up the ropes, the rhinos were startled, and they plunged about, getting rope twined round their legs. Bartlett at once ordered the release of the ropes to prevent the animals becoming further entangled and still more frightened and enraged. Then, picking up a large loaf he walked between the threshing beasts and put pieces of bread into their mouths. This steadied them and they followed Bartlett, taking pieces of bread from his hand, and the keepers were given the chance to pick up the ropes again. But the steady walk at which the party set off up the road soon increased to a trot, and then to a gallop, until Bartlett was at full stretch, dropping bits of bread like a frock-coated Milanion pursued by a very large and ugly pair of Atalantas, and the keepers on the ropes were tossed about in all directions as they vainly tried to check the pace. Bartlett shot through the open gate of the new rhino enclosure, dropped the remaining bread, and scrambled over the fence to safety

Bartlett leading rhinos

while the keeper slammed the gate shut behind the new occupants.

Trouble with pachyderms

In 1874 Jim, the famous Indian rhinoceros, normally well-behaved and a great public favourite, suddenly set upon two keepers who were cleaning out his cage and who had neglected to ensure that Jim was shut securely in his outside enclosure. So unexpected was the vicious onslaught that both men were quickly rendered unconscious and at the mercy of imminent further attack. Fortunately their first cries of alarm were heard by Scott, who rushed in and, armed only with a small whip, beat off the enraged animal and dragged the two victims to safety.

The rhinos also posed novel surgical problems to Bartlett because of trouble with their horns, which contain no bone but are composed of a very hard-packed mass of hair. On several occasions he had to devise a method of removing a horn which was damaged or malformed and a menace to the animal's health. Such operations, like many carried out at the Zoo, had a double criterion for success: the survival of the patient and the survival of the surgeon. Bartlett described such an operation to remove a horn from a female rhinoceros:[1] 'The animal became comparatively sociable and friendly, allowing me to rub her eyes with my hand, and at the same time I practised with a walking stick the process of sawing the horn. This performance I continued to go through on several mornings. Finding she submitted gently to this treatment I went one morning prepared with a sharp saw, and, with the aid of one of the keepers, who smoothed her eye in order to keep it closed, I commenced to saw off the horn, which I very effectively accomplished in about ten minutes, during which time she remained perfectly quiet. I have kept this horn, and, although it has got very dry, it weighs 11lbs., and measures 15 inches in length.'

When Obaysch the hippopotamus broke one of his big teeth Bartlett decided that it must be extracted lest it decay and cause the animal serious trouble. A powerful pair of forceps more than two feet long was made to Bartlett's design. There was no difficulty in persuading the patient to open wide his huge mouth; the problem was to avoid him snapping it shut at an inconvenient moment. After a tremendous struggle the tooth was removed, and Bartlett concluded his account with scientific detachment: 'One of the most remarkable circumstances appeared to me to be the enormous force of the air when blown from the dilated nostrils of the great beast whilst enraged. It came against me with such a force as quite surprised me. I was equally surprised to find that the furious charge he made against the iron-barred gateway was sufficient to loosen the brickwork by which the gate was held, for had the gate at that moment fallen, I should have been crushed beneath it.'

Compared with this dental operation, Bartlett must have regarded as fairly straightforward the kidnapping of the baby hippo. He noticed that soon after its birth the mother seemed to be uneasy and the little creature to be ailing, so he decided to remove the baby and give it intensive care. The mother was known to be particularly antagonistic towards the spray of water from the keeper's hose when he cleaned the cage. So, waiting until she had wandered a little distance away from her baby, the hose was played on her to distract her while Bartlett rushed into the enclosure and, rather like Tom the Piper's Son, made off with the little hippo under his arm. He wrote, 'The feat of picking up and carrying the young one was not quite so easily

Bartlett stealing the baby hippo

managed as I had anticipated. I was astonished to find that the little beast was nearly 100 lbs. in weight, and as slippery and slimy as an eel; added to this, it struggled considerably in my arms.'

Trouble with pachyderms

There is something deceptively immobile and peaceful about a hippo lying in his pool at the Zoo with the low wet mound of his back just showing above the water and eyes and nostrils poking up separately in front like little rocky outcrops. On land he can move at a fair speed, made all the more impressive by his huge bulk. To face the charge of an angry hippo with its enormous jaws gaping to show the powerful teeth must make the victim—who may well know the beast to be vegetarian—feel like a ripe tomato beneath the descending cutter of a potato chipper. It is perhaps questionable whether this was precisely the feeling of the boy who one day burst into Bartlett's office, but there was no doubt that he was terrified as he shouted that there was a hippo loose in the Gardens outside. Bartlett hurried out and posted staff to prevent members of the public straying into the beast's path, and just as he was considering how to arrange the recapture he met Scott. The hippo was known to detest Scott, and would rush furiously forward to the railings of its enclosure whenever Jumbo's keeper passed. Bartlett describes[2] how he was at once struck with an idea: '"Scott," said I, "if you go round and call at him he will come after you, but make sure he doesn't catch you; you must run into his house and up the steps onto the platform, and we will follow up and shut the door after he gets in." Scott was delighted at the idea and, with a broad grin upon his face, carried out my instructions with full and complete success.'

At the learned meetings of the Zoological Society Bartlett looked scholarly and patriarchal. The Fellows could consider themselves lucky to have found a man who embodied these qualities together with courage and a certain combination of athleticism and handyman ingenuity which seemed essential to the everyday success and safety of a Superintendent, and to a certain extent of

Copy of Letter sent to Mr Salv[illegible]

Zoological Society's Gardens.
Regent's Park.
London. N.W.

166

July 8th 1869

Dear Sir,

The outer doors to the New Elephant House are useless, the African Elephant has punched the sheet iron full of holes & the door has gone to splinters, the Rhinoceros has shown us that he can push the doors open from the outside. I shall be glad to see you as soon as you can conveniently spare time to come.

Yours faithfully

(Signed) A. D. Bartlett

A. Salvin Esq

a keeper. Bartlett and Scott certainly needed all their proven courage and ingenuity when, in 1880, Jumbo, the biggest of all the big beasts, began to play up.

Trouble with pachyderms

Jumbo was then probably just over twenty years old and of an enormous size. His lapse into bad behaviour was no surprise to Bartlett, who believed that all male elephants of this age became troublesome and dangerous. Jumbo seemed to take particular exception to his house, smashing the doors and walls with his feet, tusks, and trunk so that it became necessary to reinforce the building with massive timber beams to prevent him from getting out. When he was having one of these rages Scott was the only keeper who dared enter the house, although strangely, and possibly significantly, Jumbo became quiet as soon as he was taken to walk in the Gardens. Bartlett wrote that he was 'perfectly well aware that this restless and frantic condition could be subdued by reducing the quantity of his food, fastening his limbs by chains, and an occasional flogging; but this treatment would have called forth a multitude of protests from kind-hearted and sensitive people, and, in all probability, would have led to those concerned appearing before the magistrates at the police court charged with cruelty . . . .'

Bartlett was a man devoted to the welfare of animals, and he proved this over and over again by the trouble, and indeed the risks, he took in the care of his charges. But as Superintendent of the Zoo he was much troubled by 'kind-hearted and sensitive people'. He praised the efforts made by so many to prevent cruelty to animals, but he had no patience with attempts to bowdlerize nature, and he despised people—he called them shuddermongers—who spread false tales of cruelty. He cited as an example of shuddermongering the story that cruel bird-fanciers put out the eyes of captured wild birds to induce them to sing. He claimed that the fallacy arose from the translation of a German account describing how newly caught nightingales were placed in a box with a white blind over the wire front so that the bird should not be alarmed by seeing people close at hand. The translation

Opposite: *Complaint to the builder of the Elephant House*

said that the birds must be blinded—meaning furnished with blinds.

The London Zoo had from its earliest days many distinguished and influential people among its regular visitors. Men like Charles Dickens, ready to write publicly[3] in praise of 'the admirable society', but equally prepared to criticise details like the lack of room, and proper surfaces for the big cats to leap on as they would in nature. But perhaps the most persistent complaint against the Zoo authorities concerned the use of live animals and birds as food, particularly in the reptile house. Bartlett was absolutely certain that the reptiles could not survive without live food, and Dickens realistically represented many people's views when his journal *Household Words* declared,[4] 'It is a painful thing to contemplate any process of killing but the boa constrictor would not eat rabbits if they were dead, and then he would die himself of starvation, so that it comes to a question of serpent's life or rabbit's life; for if you keep one you sacrifice the other.'

Serious discussion of this aspect of Zoo life and death gradually, and properly, shifted from concern about the natural behaviour of snakes and alligators to concern about the character of the mixed crowd which attended the spectacle. Bartlett recognised that many of the children who found themselves present were fascinated and shocked with horror and fright. He attempted to substitute for the white mice used—which the children identified with their own pets—ordinary house mice which infested all parts of the Zoo and which apparently the children were expected to view as pests whose lowly station fitted them for consumption. But these wild mice were altogether too cunning, many of them succeeded in gnawing their way out of the snakes' cages leaving holes through which dangerous specimens escaped. Anstey, another Victorian author, writing in *The Times* after Dickens died, drew attention to the unhealthy behaviour of adults who went to great trouble to see the last moments of frogs, mice, rats, and pigeons, pushing to get a good view and even, it was suspected, occasionally bribing keepers to include

Scott and Jumbo

a larger animal such as a kid in the meal. It was thanks to such exposure in the newspapers that it was recognised that the error lay in making it easy for the vulnerable and the brutal alike to witness such a spectacle—and this unpleasant element of Zoo entertainment was removed.

Jumbo's behaviour—which Bartlett felt he could have controlled, albeit with the use of 'necessary cruelty'—got very much worse during 1880 and 1881. So violent were his attacks upon his house that he drove holes in the iron plates in the walls, but in so doing he broke off both his tusks close to the jawbone inside the mouth. Tusks continue to grow all through an elephant's life and consequently the broken ends pushed forward into the flesh of Jumbo's face and produced abscesses just below each of his eyes. Bartlett described the action he thought necessary: 'It was evident to everyone that the painful irritation caused the beast much suffering, and he fed but little and was losing flesh. He was getting so weak that he appeared afraid to lie down, and had he done so it is doubtful if he would have had strength to get up again. Upon my going to him he would allow me to put my hand upon these swellings, and appeared to me by the motion of his trunk to indicate the seat or cause of his suffering. I therefore determined to cut through the thick skin in order to discharge the accumulated pus and enable the tusks to grow out of this opening. In order to accomplish this I had a steel rod made about 18 inches in length, formed with a sharp hook at the end, the hook being flattened on the inner edge as sharp as a razor. With this instrument Scott, the keeper, and I entered the den, having previously fastened the doors of the house to prevent anyone entering and disturbing our proceedings, as I was fearful that the noise made by the other keepers would alarm the brute or cause him to be restless. Standing under his lower jaw and passing the instrument above the swollen part, I, with a sharp pull, hooking fast into the skin, cut it through, causing a most frightful discharge of very offensive matter; the poor beast uttered a loud shriek and rushed from us, bleeding, shaking and trembling, but without exhibiting any anger. After a little coaxing and talking to, he allowed us to wash out the wound by syringing it with water. On the following morning we determined to operate upon the other abscess on the opposite side. We had, however,

Attacking the doors of his house

some misgiving as to the result of our second attempt to operate upon him, but, to our intense surprise, the beast stood perfectly still until the sudden cut caused him to start and give another cry like the one he uttered the day before. The improvement in the animal's condition after these two operations was most remarkable; the tusks soon made their appearance growing through the apertures that had been cut for the discharge of the abscesses.'

Although Jumbo's health improved, his behaviour did not, and Bartlett attributed this to the emotional state known as *musth*[5] which affects all male and some female elephants periodically during their adult life. An elephant on *musth* is usually irritable, excitable, and violent to the point of being extremely dangerous. This state had been well known for very many years among elephants in captivity and it was usually believed that *musth* was in some way related to a kind of sexual rhythm which was particularly pronounced in the adult male.

A modern authority on elephants[6] has suggested that Jumbo's recalcitrant behaviour might not have been due to the mysterious sexual rhythm of *musth* but, more prosaically, to the sort of painful tooth-ache that makes babies ill-tempered to the point of frenzy and their parents dull-eyed with loss of sleep.

The elephant lives on a diet of soft vegetable material and it has twenty-four massive molar teeth to grind up this food—six in each jawbone. When it is very young the elephant has three of the six molars in use and as it gets older these first three teeth wear out successively and a fourth moves forward in the jaw. When this begins to wear, the fifth molar moves forward to take on the grinding task, and finally when the sixth and last molar has moved into place and worn out, the old elephant can no longer chew the hundred and fifty pounds or so of food it requires daily and it will die.

The first molars are quite small—about the size of a man's top thumb joint—and the second, third, etc., are progressively larger, until the sixth molar is about the size of a clenched fist. The fourth molars move into position when the calf is about five years old, the fifth erupt when the elephant is between fifteen and twenty, and the sixth at about thirty years of age. The growth of these teeth, and in particular the forward movement of the large molars in the bony tissue in which they are embedded causes considerable mechanical stress in the jaw. At these fairly well defined times in its life the elephant is likely to experience much pain and irritation: it is subject to teething troubles, but on the grand scale, and it is correspondingly fractious. Sylvia Sikes writes[7] of Jumbo, 'It is interesting that the period in which he proved so difficult to handle at the London Zoo must have been just about the time when his fifth molars were erupting in each half-jaw.'

Lancing the abcesses

The fact that the African elephant in captivity is undoubtedly more troubled than the Indian by these unsettled periods, and is generally more intractable, may possibly be due simply to the fact that his teeth give him more trouble. Certainly, although in each case there are six molars which erupt in succession, there are very significant differences between the size and shape of the teeth in the two species. It is also sometimes suggested that in captivity the rarer African elephant may be hungry because it is given the same rations as the smaller Indian elephant, but it is difficult to believe that Bartlett and a doting public would have kept Jumbo short either of his proper balanced diet or his supplementary packing of buns. A third possible explanation advanced for the elephant's irritability is that it comes to miss the sociability of the herd roaming free in the wild. If there is any validity in such a suggestion it would be particularly pertinent to animals kept under old-fashioned conditions in Zoos where their existence included a large measure of lonely confinement which would perhaps be especially irksome to a fully mature male African bush elephant. It is possibly significant that Jumbo's violent tantrums invariably subsided when he was taken out of his house to walk in the Gardens.

Whatever the reasons for Jumbo's continued violent phases, and it is likely that there were more than one, Bartlett was haunted by the thought that Jumbo would end sixteen years of gentleness, during which he had given infinite pleasure to the public, by some dreadful outburst which would kill or maim scores of children and other visitors in the crowded Gardens. Only Scott could now control Jumbo in one of his periodic rages. This was a situation which had to a large extent been cultivated by Scott himself, who had always refused to have an under-keeper and was so fiercely possessive of his great charge—and the tips he earned—that most of the Zoo staff were nearly as frightened of Scott as they were of Jumbo.

Jumbo was withdrawn from riding during these phases of ill humour so that Bartlett was at least spared the nervous tension of seeing him lumbering among the crowds, a

Zoological Gardens
N W
12th March 1882

Miss Stevens

The Size round Jumbo s
hind feet measures 5 feet
And the fore feet 5 feet 6
Yours greatly obliged

Matthew Scott

Jumbo s Keeper

huge miracle of gentleness and affability to those who thronged round him, but to Bartlett as menacing as some great mountain with a wisp of smoke at its peak. In December 1881 the Superintendent, remembering no doubt from his childhood the difficulty in destroying Chunee when he ran amok and devastated his quarters in the Strand Menagerie, sought[8] and obtained from the Council permission to buy an elephant gun against the possibility that, with Scott ill or otherwise absent, Jumbo should prove impossible to control in one of his attacks.

Then out of the blue in 1882 came an opportunity for Bartlett to be forever free from the worry that Jumbo would cause some disaster, to be free too from the possibility of being stigmatized as the man who destroyed the nation's favourite. It was hardly surprising that the Superintendent should recommend to the Council of the London Zoological Society that they accept a cash offer for Jumbo. Barnum wanted to buy him and ship him to the United States.

Letter and picture in child's scrapbook

Rally to Jumbo's defence

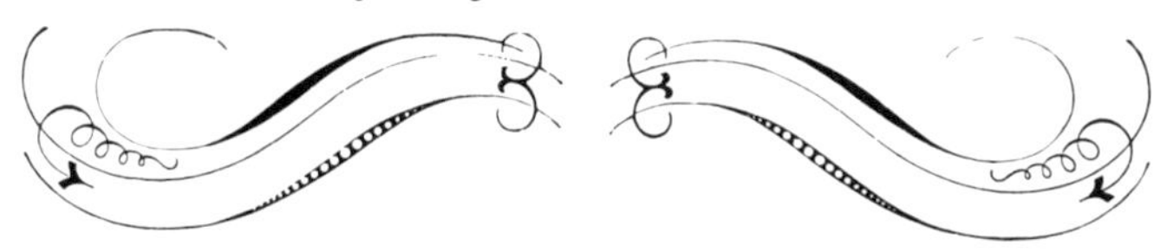

Phineas Taylor Barnum, the Great American Showman, Total Abstainer, Church Elder, and self-styled Prince of Humbugs, was a master of ballyhoo. On his Connecticut farm the plough was pulled by an elephant, which was in no way a necessary item of agricultural economy but was an amusing diversion for Barnum's family and friends, justified, like a modern sponsored sports event, by the publicity said to be generated for the business. That business was the Circus, the lusty, rip-roaring, pack-them-in-and-move-on style of show business which was Barnum's vocation. There was fierce competition from rivals, and if the crowds were to be kept flocking to The Greatest Show on Earth then more daring acts, more spectacular displays, and more amazing exhibits had continually to be sought out by the agents of the man who had already given the public the opportunity to pay to see the Feejee Mermaid, and General Tom Thumb. Occasionally the problem was not to get the customers in, but to get them out. When they lingered too long in the menagerie with the result that people crowding the entrance were unable to pay their money and be admitted, Barnum improved the flow by putting up an excitingly large sign which read 'This Way To The Egress'.

In 1881 Barnum's agents were in Europe looking for first-class attractions for his menagerie, and they let it be known in the great Zoos of England, France, and Germany that they were only interested in major purchases. What

Phineas T. Barnum

they had in mind they said was, say, twenty giraffes or thirty ostriches or 'a big lot of something'.[1] There was no question of surplus stock on this scale being available at the London Zoo, or indeed anywhere else in Europe, but Barnum's men did manage to get hold of seven giraffes in Germany and ship them back to the United States.

Rally to Jumbo's defence

While they were going about their business of buying animals or hiring circus acts Barnum's employees, wherever they went, were expected to keep their ears open for rumours and travellers' tales which might lead to the uncovering of some 'raree' which could be put on show. The least perspicacious of agents could hardly have spent any time with the officials at Regent's Park in 1881 without getting wind of the fact that though Jumbo might be the most famous animal in the world and the public's pet, he was no favourite with the staff at the Zoo, and a tremendous worry to the Superintendent and the Council. When Barnum's agents got back to the United States they thought it worth mentioning this state of affairs to their employer, who had seen Jumbo several times on visits to London and had coveted him for years.

Barnum wasted no time and at once got in touch with Bartlett to say that he would be prepared to buy Jumbo if the Council were willing, and their terms reasonable. The Council were shaken by this audacious proposal which they would have dismissed with ridicule a year earlier. But now they actually had before them Bartlett's dreadful request for an elephant gun that might any day make the Zoo's biggest crowd puller into a mountain of catsmeat, and themselves into the most reviled body in the country. This unsought opportunity to be rid of their worry at a handsome profit was too attractive to be missed. After some discussion Barnum was told that the Zoo's price was two thousand pounds, and early in 1882 he replied by cable, 'I accept your offer; my agents will be with you in a few days.'

The negotiations had been private and the first time the public—and many Fellows of the Zoological Society—heard of the transaction was when *The Times* of 25 January

1882 published a piece under the heading *The Great African Elephant*: 'Barnum, the American showman, has bought for the sum of £2000, the large male African Elephant, which has for many years formed one of the principal attractions in the Gardens of the Zoological Society in the Regent's Park.

'The purchase has been made upon the understanding that the animal is to be shipped to America at the risk of the purchaser. To those who know the size, weight, and strength of this ponderous creature (certainly the largest elephant in Europe), the undertaking is one of serious difficulty and not unattended with some danger.'

In view of what subsequently occurred, it was quite remarkable that there was practically no public reaction to this announcement for nearly three weeks. It was like the unnatural quiet between star-shell and barrage. The public outcry only burst in all its violence when Barnum's men arrived at the Zoo on Friday, 17 February 1882 with the large crate in which Jumbo was to be carried to the London Docks and placed on board the *Persian Monarch*, due to sail for the United States on the Sunday.

On Tuesday, 21 February 1882 a letter appeared in *The Times*:

> Sir,
>
> An attempt was made on Saturday to remove a distinguished and, by children, a much-loved resident from London, but, happily, without success.
>
> I allude to Jumbo, the great and docile elephant who has for very many years been one of the chief attractions of the Zoological Gardens, but who for reasons difficult to understand, has lately been sold to an American showman.
>
> In common with many other Fellows of the Society, I have found my disgust at this sale intensified by the pathetic and almost human distress of the poor animal at the attempted separation of him from his home and his family.
>
> Our hearts are not harder than those of his keepers,

Rally to Jumbo's defence

and for his own sake, as well as for that of the rising generation, I venture to ask if it is too late to annul the bargain?

If his price be needful to the funds of our Society, I think it would be easy to raise the sum by subscription among the many who feel, with

Your obedient servant,

A PENITENT FELLOW

It seems likely that the English people, silent for nearly three weeks after the sale of Jumbo was announced, might apathetically have accepted that this was a commercial transaction, satisfying vendor and buyer, and therefore a matter in which the public had no more right nor cause to interfere than in the export of an art treasure from a private collection to the United States. Had the operation gone as slickly as Barnum's agents planned, then Jumbo would have been in his box and on the high seas bound for New York before Tuesday's *Times* was published with 'Penitent Fellow's' letter. Indeed the letter might never have been written had it not been for 'the pathetic and almost human distress of the poor animal'. It was Jumbo's

Barnum instructing General Tom Thumb

own behaviour which was the cause of the *Persian Monarch* slipping down the Thames to sea with a vacant space in her specially prepared hold where Jumbo's crate should have stood, while that crate waited empty outside the elephant house at the Zoo and the great animal was fed buns by his London friends. It was Jumbo's manifest and continued refusal to leave the Zoo which rallied the public to his support.

On Friday, 17 February 1882 Barnum's men, Mr Davis and William Newman—'Elephant Bill' of the circus—had arrived at the Zoo with the crate in which they proposed to remove Jumbo to the London Docks the next day. Their arrival was not unnoticed, and details of the box which was to contain Jumbo for over a fortnight on the voyage were published without comment in the London press.[2] The crate, rather like a very large horse-box, was strongly made of pitch pine planking, lined and reinforced with oak, and bound together with massive iron straps firmly bolted into place. It was about fourteen feet long, eight feet wide, and twelve feet high, so there was very little room for movement, certainly not enough for an elephant to turn around, although he might be able to sit down. The horizontal planks making up the ends of the box were to be fixed in position after Jumbo was installed, and they left a gap of about three feet at the top in front through which he would be able to see and to extend his trunk if he wished.

On the Saturday morning the banker's draft for £2000 was handed over and in the Zoo's Daily Occurrence Book the sale was recorded of '1 African Elephant ♂. Received in exchange June 26 1865'. A few modifications were made to the crate at Bartlett's suggestion to make it stronger, and then it was put on a very heavy trolley with thick squat wheels. These wheels rested on a short iron track laid in a trench dug deep enough to ensure that the ramp up which Jumbo would have to walk to enter the box was not too steep.

Jumbo had now passed officially into the hands of the Americans who, under the terms of sale, had bought him 'as he stands'. It was their responsibility to get him out of the Gardens and onto the ship. Bartlett and Scott had no idea how Newman proposed to tackle the task, but it was soon clear that he was a man who believed in strong measures, and one who would stand for no nonsense from an animal in his charge. His first move was to attach Jumbo's front feet separately by long chains to some strong rails.[3] Scott assisted with this and the animal was puzzled and a little disturbed as this unaccustomed restraint was fastened on him by his old friend. At first he examined the unwelcome chains quietly with his trunk, then he began to jerk and pull his legs away from them, and when this did not free his feet he repeatedly picked up a loop of chain in his trunk and dropped it heavily on the ground as though to break it.

Rally to Jumbo's defence

But this was only a beginning to Jumbo's unhappiness. Newman now ordered very heavy chain to be run over the elephant's head, round his body and between his legs, like a horse's martingale. These chains were eventually to be fixed to the inside of the crate so that he would be held firmly in place during all the lifting and moving that would be necessary before he was on board the ship. Poor Jumbo became very frightened at so much chain clanking and rubbing all over his body. He roared and

Chaining Jumbo

he plunged and he bellowed, and it was some time before his agitation had sufficiently subsided for him to be led up the ramp to the entrance of the crate. But as soon as he got his front feet to the top of the ramp he sensed a trap ahead and at once lay down flat on his stomach with his hind legs stretched out behind him. No matter how much he was pushed and cajoled he would advance no further and he was thoroughly upset and frightened. Again and again he was led away from the box and walked around for a while, but each time he was brought back to the ramp he refused to mount it and enter the crate.

When night fell on the Saturday there was no progress, except that Jumbo was now looped in heavy chain which made the worried creature look particularly pathetic. At midnight Newman ordered a change of plan. The eight Pickford's horses which had been standing by all day to haul Jumbo away were now called in to take the empty crate on its trolley to St. Katharine Dock, near the Tower. The new plan was that Jumbo should be walked through the streets five or six miles to the Dock, leaving the Zoo at

Refusing to mount the ramp

5 a.m. on the Sunday. It was hoped that by the time he arrived at the quay he would be so tired that he would be glad to enter his box to rest, and could then be rushed on board the *Persian Monarch* which was to sail on the tide later that day.

Rally to Jumbo's defence

Word had got round of trouble at the Zoo, and when Scott led Jumbo, in chains, out of the Gardens at dawn on the Sunday morning there was a large crowd gathered outside. Jumbo came through the gates onto the public

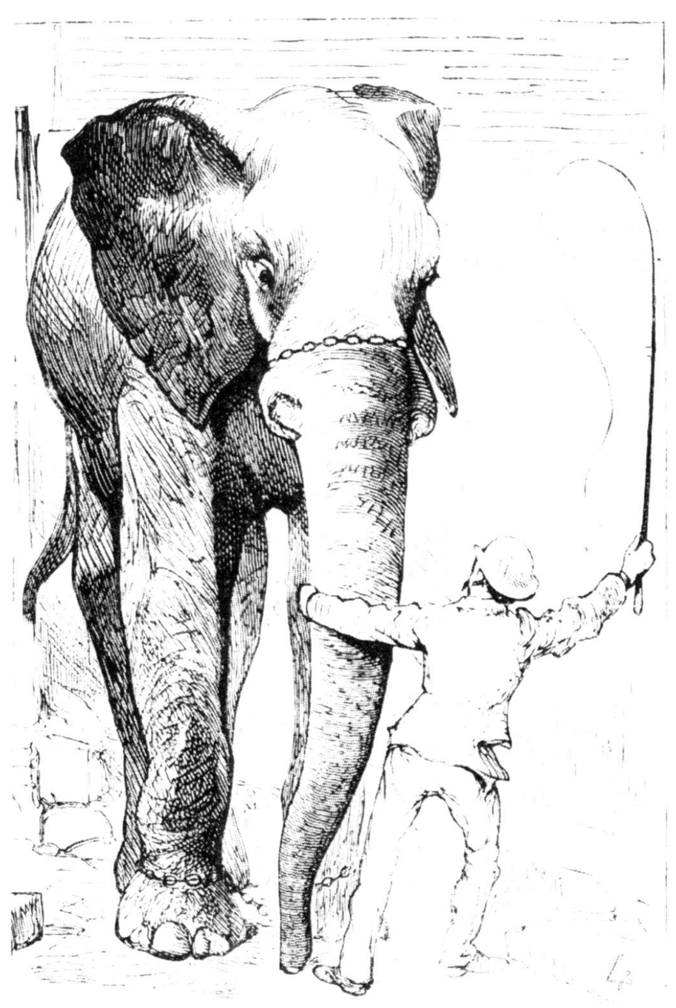

Playing up

road and at once knelt down. Nothing that Scott or Newman said or did would make him go any further forward. He did not seem to be angry or frightened, but perfectly good-tempered. Occasionally he lifted his trunk to give a trumpet call which brought a response from the elephants in the Gardens behind him, but otherwise he was very well-behaved except that he would not move away from the Zoo.

Eventually, when it was clear that there was no chance of getting him to the docks in time to catch the ship, Scott ordered the elephant to walk back into the Gardens. Jumbo instantly and happily obeyed, and when the Fellows and their friends came into the Zoo later that Sunday he was there, still in his chains, but standing in his old enclosure ready as always to receive gifts of buns and fruit.

The crowd outside the Zoo had been much affected by the sight of Jumbo kneeling in chains, apparently unwilling to leave his home and friends. When he was led back into the Gardens the mob cheered, and many of them cherished the moment as a triumph for an honest British underdog over the pushing Yankees. This sentimental story with jingoistic undertones was correctly recognised by the Press as likely to capture the public imagination. The reports of Jumbo's brave resistance excited further public concern, which in turn justified

Not another step

Submission

Rally to Jumbo's defence

even more printed news and comment, until very quickly the sensation craved by the Press, and Barnum, and the readers, was achieved. A wreath of flowers, big enough to go around Jumbo's neck, was delivered at the Zoo to be worn as 'a trophy of triumph over his brutal owners and American kidnappers'.[4] *Animal World*, the monthly paper of the RSPCA, reported, 'One man, who ought to be fined, christened his son "Jumbo", thereby condemning him to be a "rough" for life.'

The Council of the Zoological Society was castigated in the correspondence and opinion columns of most newspapers and journals with a directness typical of the period, and with an intensity of indignation and emotion which flows rarely from an Englishman's pen except in such matters as sport and the welfare of animals and trees. The first attacks concentrated upon the cruel fate to which Jumbo had been so callously consigned. That the animal would suffer fear and unhappiness when removed from familiar surroundings to face a long and uncomfortable journey was undeniable, but the old fiction of an attachment between Jumbo and Alice, the Zoo's other African elephant, was now further exaggerated to add even more pathos to the story. Alice was referred to as his wife—sometimes as his pregnant wife—and it was said that her unhappy cries when Jumbo was first led in chains out of the gates of the Gardens had made him even more frantic as he lay in the road and refused to be led to the docks.

A leader in one London paper[5] set the style of the campaign by referring to the popular works of Mrs Harriet Beecher Stowe and declaring that 'the scene reminds us of Mr Selby disposing of Uncle Tom'.

Lying in the road

One of what the *Illustrated London News*[6] called its 'numerous correspondents, chiefly ladies,[7] protested that the sale of Jumbo was a disgraceful transaction and expressed her astonishment that 'for the sake of two thousand pounds the Royal (*sic*) Zoological Society should sell this wonderful and faithful old friend into the hands of a travelling showman'. The *Pall Mall Gazette*[7] continued the theme: 'Is this the way we recompense our oldest friends, these best benefactors who have given us the one boon which is without alloy—hearty and innocent enjoyment?'

Jumbo wins. Back into the Zoo

Rally to Jumbo's defence

The shame and indignation felt at what was regarded as disgraceful ingratitude and cruelty to an animal friend was taken up in all types of paper and was further inflamed when the *Daily Telegraph*,[8] strongly and emotionally pro-Jumbo, stated, 'Mr William Newman, "Elephant Bill", conceives he has the right to shoot Jumbo if necessary. "Living or dead," he declares, "Jumbo is to go to New York."'

Many of the letters and articles dwelt upon the sorrow of the children who loved Jumbo, and the deprivation of many thousands—some unborn—who would now never experience the pleasure and excitement of a ride on his back. The children themselves, prompted or not, wrote to the papers, to the Zoo, even to Barnum. When a whole school petitioned the Zoological Society, the Secretary replied,[9] 'Dear Friends, Your petition has been duly received, but I fear we shall not be able to assent to your request. We must ask you to believe that our Superintendent knows better what elephants are suitable to be kept in the Society's Gardens than you do. There are still three elephants left in the Gardens, upon which we hope you will have many rides in the future.'

Barnum claimed that hundreds of English children had written him letters, one of which he published:[10]

> I write in behalf of our dear old Jumbo. Do be kind and generous to our English boys and girls. We do so love him, and I am sure if you have children or little friends of your own you will be able to understand how their hearts would ache and their tears be shed should they lose the friend who has given them such delight, and who is one of their few pleasures in this great and sorrowful city. We all know, from older and cleverer heads, that by rights, Jumbo is yours, as you have paid the money for him; but, dear Mr Barnum, you, who have so many famous animals, and among them so many elephants, surely will think seriously and kindly before you take from us our very dear friend Jumbo . . . . I think, indeed I do not think, I am sure, that if Jumbo had

> been our purchase from you, and letters had been sent to us telling of the sorrow of American children at parting with an old favorite, every English girl and boy, man and woman, would have said with one voice, that the purchase money should be given back, and the animal left to delight the children across the Atlantic . . . . You may think it a waste of time for a young girl to write to you when older and wiser heads have failed, but I must tell you of the thousands of children to whom the parting from Jumbo will be a terrible grief. Be to us the generous hearted man you are believed to be and give us back our Jumbo.

There is a remarkable precociousness about the letter which in style, and indeed in the spelling of 'favorite', more readily evokes the picture of a Barnum copy-writer than 'A Young English Girl' which was the signature at the end.

Punch, which referred to Jumbo in text and picture two or three times in each issue at this time, published a children's lament to be sung to the tune of a popular song of the time.[11]

The Cry of the Children
(A propos of Jumbo)

Air: 'If I had a donkey wot wouldn't go.'

If *I* owned Jumbo
(Who declines to go)
Would I sell him to a Show?
No, no, not I.
When the Titan I saw
Firmly planted his paw,
I would shout 'HOORAW'
For his bra-ve-ry.

Chorus.
If an army of Yankees should proffer their pay,
I'd button my pockets, and send them away.

Rally to Jumbo's defence

What forget all the fun?
All the tricks he has done?
The ride and the bun?
No, no, not I.
At so sorry a turn
Every bosom must burn
And the notion spurn
Of such cru-el-ty.

Chorus.
Though a legion of Fellows might say their say,
I'd decline to part with our pet for pay.

Not all the published comment was at the lowest popular level of sentimentality. *The Spectator*'s views[12] were more realistic and its criticism restrained:

> Have not the Managers of the Gardens been a little hasty in selling such a beast? We think nothing of the children's letters to the papers, though they are very natural, for New York children want amusement and instruction as much as Londoners, nor much of the complaint that Jumbo would evidently rather stay. So would the grand bull of ducal pedigree who goes next week to Australia, and the grander mare who came last week from Tunis, and had, perhaps, lived in a tent half her life; and so also would conscripts, naval officers, and Cetewayo. One must subordinate private feelings of that kind to the general good, and it is for elephants' general good that they should be greatly sought after and fetch high prices and draw great crowds, and so justify careful feeding, good treatment, and generous keep, otherwise their only destiny would be knife-handles. But still, have not the Managers of the Gardens been a little hasty? . . . it is nearly certain that in another century, when Jumbo has arrived at a green old age—elephants are believed to live 150 years, and certainly live above 130—the animal will, with the exception of the few in confinement, have totally ceased to exist. There are not, and will not be, 10,000,000 elephants to

> supply the century's demand, while every rise in the price of ivory and every improvement in communication will increase the severity of the hunt. When 'Jumbo' is alone in the world, as he very possibly will be, he will be worth thousands, and be for naturalists an object of almost as much interest as a moa . . . . It is a pity, in the interest of science as well as of the Gardens, to send him away.

Correspondents pointed out[13] that elephants did not live as long as *The Spectator* stated, but the point about the value of Jumbo as a scientific specimen was pursued. *The Saturday Review* wrote,[14]

> There was a time when the Zoological Society was willing to give large sums—thousands of pounds, in fact—ungrudgingly for specimens of rare animals, as in the case of the four giraffes obtained by M. Thibaut in 1835, and the hippopotamus—the first brought to this country—in 1850. It seems therefore, to say the least, odd that they should be willing to sacrifice such a unique specimen as Jumbo for a sum of money which must really be a bagatelle for them. Indeed the question of profit and loss can hardly enter into their transactions; for their present income is quite sufficient to enable them, as a scientific body, to carry out all the provisions of their charter, under which a grant was made to them of a large portion of one of the best London Parks. Were they a mere trading body, such a concession could never have been made.

In the face of the public outcry, and some private criticism within the Zoological Society, the Secretary, Sclater, published an account of the sale[15] saying, 'It was, however, hoped that the Fellows of the Society and others would have been satisfied that the Council were acting for the best, and would not have required any detailed statement of the motives by which the Council were guided in this transaction . . . .' He referred particularly

Rally to Jumbo's defence

to the risk of Jumbo running amok in the Gardens, and pointed out that the menagerie of Barnum, Bailey, and Hutchinson contained more than twenty elephants, including two calves born in captivity, and that it had facilities not available at Regent's Park for withdrawing an excitable elephant into seclusion away from the public. A member of the Council angrily referred to the criticism directed at that body as misrepresentation. He pointed out[16] that no one had disputed the Council's discretion in parting with elephants on two previous occasions, in 1854 and 1873, but went on, 'certainly neither of them was called "Jumbo", a name which has clearly done much to foster the present agitation. If our "Jumbo" had been called by some name as unpronounceable as that of the two Indian Elephants now in the Society's possession, we should have heard much less of his virtues.'

It was of course unimaginable that Barnum should not take a part in the wrangle. A cliff-hanger serial story, an appealing animal, the pleas of little children, a row in a learned society, national pride, the passionate interest of the highest and the lowest in the land, all these elements of the Jumbo affair were just the things that a good-living publicist would crave more than manna in a heavenly Madison Avenue. Barnum wanted to make sure that the fiery controversy lit up his name. He tried to keep it crackling and to direct it where it would best serve his highly individual ideas of advertisement. The Editor of The *Daily Telegraph* sent him a cable, asking on what terms he would sell Jumbo back, and ending, perhaps unwisely, 'Answer prepaid, unlimited.' Barnum could not resist it. In a sentence he dismissed the question of relinquishing Jumbo,[17] and then went on at considerable length, and at the *Daily Telegraph*'s expense, with what amounted to a comprehensive advertisement of the delights of the Barnum Four Ring Circus and its future programme.

While sentimental pleading and intellectual jousting filled the newspaper columns a sterner battle of wits and strength was going on at the Zoo between Jumbo and those who were trying to crate him. Whenever he was brought to the point of entering his box, Jumbo would stand stock still, kneel down, or lie flat. His usual amiable obedience would switch abruptly to apparently total intractability at every crucial point in the preparations for his departure. As the days slipped by and it began to appear possible that Jumbo might once again miss a booked passage to New York, Bartlett and Elephant Bill Newman found themselves suspecting that the battle was not between man and elephant alone, but that Jumbo's uncharacteristic disobedience in this one matter might be partly, even entirely, the result of human intervention—deliberate sabotage by someone who wished to keep Jumbo in London and who had the power of command over him.

The keepers in 1882 were men of considerable independence and, although their official wages were not large, those who had charge of popular exhibits could count on tips, particularly from favoured visitors who had perhaps been given a spicy lecture, conducted personally round the animals, allowed to hold a snake, or granted some other such privilege. Keepers in charge of riding animals—camels or elephants—were specially well placed to receive such tips. The Zoo made no charge for these rides, but when the lucky children were lifted down by the keeper and returned to their parents it was customary for some small coin, usually silver, to change hands—or occasionally to pass from hand to trunk to pocket. The biggest treat of all was a ride on the great Jumbo's back, and Scott's gratuities were correspondingly generous. It is possible to get some idea of the value of the tips from the fact that, immediately after Jumbo's time at the Zoo, twopenny tickets were issued for elephant rides, and the proceeds, which were shared between the keepers and the Zoological Society, came to between fifty and a hundred pounds a month.[18] However rough the arithmetic, there is little doubt that Scott's position as Jumbo's keeper gave him a very good income, as well as the satisfaction of prestige among his fellow employees at the Zoo, and the admiration of the crowds of visitors in the Gardens. To find that this pleasant and remunerative life was about to be shattered by the removal of the great elephant he had looked after for seventeen years must have been very disturbing.

Rally to Jumbo's defence

When an elephant and its keeper have been constantly together for such a long period the *rapport* between them is likely to have become very close indeed. In particular the elephant will understand the keeper's commands so well that it will respond to gestures which are too slight to be noticed even by careful observers. Both Bartlett and Newman suspected that when Jumbo had knelt in the road or been otherwise obstructive it was in response to some secret signal from Scott.[19] Bartlett wrote, 'this caused me to ask Newman whether if I removed Scott from the elephant-house, he would undertake the charge of the beast himself. This he at once consented to do. Having arranged this matter, I proceeded with Newman to the elephant-house, and calling Scott outside, told him that it was my intention to send him away from the Gardens for a time in order that Newman should get accustomed to the habits and management of Jumbo before he left England. At the same time I remarked to Scott that Mr Barnum had made him a most liberal offer if he would accompany the animal to America, and his place would be kept open for him here should he return in a specified time. Scott immediately begged me not to carry out my intention of giving him a holiday, stating that if I would give him another day he would do his best to induce Jumbo to enter his box . . . .'

This did the trick. The next day Jumbo became remarkably more cooperative and the arrangements for his departure proceeded smoothly, it being agreed that Scott should be granted six months leave of absence from the Zoo to accompany him. It was a great relief to Newman and his helpers, who had grown increasingly tense and irritable at being made foolish in the eyes of a delighted public who vociferously supported Jumbo in what they were pleased to regard as his gallant lone resistance.

Barnum, in New York, heard with shrewd equanimity about his men's difficulties. When the first unsuccessful attempt was made to walk Jumbo out of the Zoo, Barnum's London agent cabled him,[20] 'Jumbo has laid down in the street and won't get up. What shall we do?' The reply was, 'Let him lie there a week if he wants to. It is the best advertisement in the world.'

Rally to Jumbo's defence

Once the goodwill of Scott—and hence of Jumbo—had been secured, new plans were made to get Jumbo in his crate in time to take passage in the second week of March. The first passage booked had been in the *Persian Monarch* which had sailed without him back in February, and now it was necessary to wait for another sailing by a ship of the Monarch Line, because it had been established that the hatch, hold, and deckhead dimensions of these vessels would admit Jumbo's crate and accommodate it satisfactorily on the trans-Atlantic crossing. There was thus plenty of time for a newly cooperative Jumbo to be trained to accept the crate; and plenty of time, too, for the cries of the 'Save Jumbo' campaign to rise even higher in pitch and intensity; for the Zoo to harvest a bumper catch-crop of admission money from extra visitors; and for the sounds of the controversy to penetrate to New York and be amplified by the Barnum publicity machine to reverberate around America and prepare that continent to welcome the new circus recruit with enthusiasm and generosity.

The new plan to box Jumbo required first that a huge pit should be dug immediately outside the door that led from his stable to the open-air enclosure. The heavy trolley designed to carry Jumbo's crate was placed in the bottom of this pit, which was four or five feet deep. One end of the pit sloped gradually upwards to ground level, and rails were laid so that the trolley could eventually be pulled up this slope. When the crate was placed on the trolley its floor came just below the level of the ground. The two ends of the crate were knocked out, the pit and sloping trench filled in with earth, and the floor of the crate also covered with a layer of earth, so that Jumbo was left with what appeared to be a wooden tube or tunnel through which he was led by Scott several times a day on the way to and from his usual excursions in the Gardens to give rides.

All this digging and carpentry and lifting and hauling

was more than Barnum's men could manage on their own. During this period the official Daily Occurrence Book records that a large fraction of the Zoo's small staff of carpenters, labourers, etc. was 'Assisting with Elephant Box'. But the authorities had no cause to look askance at the cost to them of this unexpected demand upon the Zoo's resources brought about by Jumbo's protracted departure arrangements, for the same daily record shows that the paying visitors were now numbered in thousands compared with the hundreds who had come into the Gardens on the corresponding dates of the previous year.

The extra cash flowing in as a result of the Jumbo affair was a pleasant surprise, but less welcome was the bright light of critical inspection now turned upon the activities of the Council, whose members regarded themselves as public-spirited men reaching decisions, in civilised and private discussion, which were in the best interests of the Zoological Society. Now, the general public, encouraged by the Press, was disrespectfully casting doubts on their wisdom and competence, while certain radical Fellows of the Society itself were seeking to question and reduce their autocratic power.

The President of the Society, speaking at a General Meeting held at the height of the controversy,[21] when Newman was making his second attempt to crate Jumbo, was particularly bitter about the attacks from within the Society: 'There is much in this which is to me a novel and painful experience; but I am told that it is what all must expect who undertake the responsibility of any kind of work for the benefit of others. However this may be in political life, it might have been hoped that among those who followed the calmer pursuits encouraged by this Society, there would not have been any found, who either openly or under cover of anonymous slander in newspaper articles, letters, and postcards, would have imputed to us, which I regret to say has been freely done, motives absolutely contrary to those by which we know we have been ever actuated.'

Opposite: *Send Bradlaugh not Jumbo*

Jumbo's cause was beginning to attract more influential

ARCADES JUMBO; OR, BR-DL-GH AND THE ELEPHANT.

(*With a profound apology to Jumbo.*)

unch (*to Barnum*). "Hail, Columbia! An Elephant's House is his Castle! Leave Jumbo alone, and Three Hundred
sand Million British Children, not to mention Billions of British Babes unborn, will bless the Name of Barnum.
t'other instead, and you will earn the Gratitude of all Parties, even that of the trusty and very much-tried
r One representing Northampton. Why, cert'nly! Love to yourself, and America generally. *Vive* Barnum!
e princeps in the Show Line—bar none. Hail, Columbia!—Yours truly, *Punch*."

interest. Questions were asked in the House of Commons. The Editor of *Vanity Fair* announced that he was starting a Jumbo Defence Fund with a personal subscription of five pounds.[22] He mentioned an Indian elephant reputed to be 'at least 124 years old', and commented, 'If Jumbo does as well as this he will probably survive the British Empire,' thus demonstrating that his political intuition as an editor was sounder than his zoological information. Ruskin, the art critic and social conscience of the Victorian middle-class, whose own poor health at this time made him only too familiar, and perhaps therefore more sympathetic, with periodic bouts of depression and ill-humour, declared,[23] 'I, for one of the said Fellows, am not in the habit of selling my old pets or parting with my old servants because I find them subject occasionally, perhaps even "periodically", to fits of ill temper; and I not only "regret" the proceedings of the Council, but disclaim them utterly as disgraceful to the City of London and dishonourable to humanity. If the Council want money let them beg it—if they want a stronger elephant's house let them build it; there is brick and iron enough in London to keep a single beast safe with, I suppose, and if there are not children in London brave enough to back him in his afternoon walk, let them look at him and go to their rocking horses.'

Bartlett must have judged it irresponsible to suggest that children should be brave enough to ride on Jumbo's back, particularly when this counsel of recklessness came from one who in his own childhood had never even ridden the most docile pony.[24]

Another powerful formative influence on English taste and opinion—the Music Hall—rallied the pit and gallery to Jumbo's side with specially composed musical pieces: *Jumbo's Jinks*, *The Jumbo and Alice Polka*, and *Why Part With Jumbo, the Pet of the Zoo.* This last piece was sung by G. H. Macdermott who specialised in songs on current affairs and who, a few years before, had put a new word into the language with his famous number *We don't want to fight, but, by Jingo, if we do.*

It was even rumoured that Queen Victoria herself, and

the Prince of Wales, had let it be known that they strongly disapproved of the sale. According to Barnum's agent, the Queen had telegraphed Bartlett for full particulars about the sale of Jumbo, and the Prince of Wales had required the Superintendent to attend upon him at Marlborough House to discuss the matter.[25] No one did more to spread these stories than Barnum, who was keen to keep good publicity going and who had entertained proprietorial feelings towards the Queen and her family ever since he had been received so appreciatively, and indeed so frequently, at Court with the twenty-five inch General Tom Thumb when he had brought the celebrated midget to England in 1844. The rumours of the Queen's concern were undoubtedly soundly based. A letter from the Colonial Secretary's private secretary to Sir Henry Ponsonby, the Queen's private secretary, ends,[26] 'I am glad to hear that H.M. takes an interest in Jumbo. The poor brute has behaved with too much dignity to be consigned to the horrible vulgarity of Barnum and his "mammoth show".'

Rally to Jumbo's defence

Alarmed by the level to which criticism had now risen, the Council of the Zoological Society thought it prudent to look again at the arrangements for Jumbo's removal, and to protect themselves from blame should there be any mishap. They commissioned an independent firm of consulting engineers and surveyors to report 'whether the means provided for carrying the Box to the Docks are such as are likely to prove safe and effectual'.[27] The consultants criticised the trolley because the iron tyres on the wheels were too narrow and 'not suitable for moving so great a load especially upon soft gravel paths and roads such as those within the Society's grounds'. They suggested certain strengthening modifications to be made to the crate which would make it satisfactory for its purpose, 'assuming the Elephant to be docile and tractable'. They went on however to warn that if 'the Animal became excited and violent, we are of opinion that the Box is not constructed so as to resist his fury and strength'. They made no proposals for the design of a box to meet this

Jumbo's lament

'extreme case . . . as we understand the Council do not propose to take any such responsibility'.

The Council now felt that they had armed themselves to face any criticism or legal action should something go wrong while Jumbo was being removed from the Gardens, but they hardly expected to have to face Court proceedings before the event took place.

In *The Times*[28] on Monday, 6 March 1882 a letter was published which informed the Editor that some of the

Rally to Jumbo's defence

JUMBO'S LAMENT

AIR—"*Why did my Master sell me?*"

O WHY did the Council sell me?
Why did 'cute BARNUM buy me?
Why did false BARTLETT doom me
To exile far away?
What did my Alice tell me?
Public with buns who ply me,
Vote me a paddock roomy,
Where I may rest or play!
Chorus—Why did the Council sell me?

Why did stern Justice CHITTY—
Man who from law ne'er flinches—
Quash ROMER's kind injunction
On my behalf? Bohoo!
Will they, devoid of pity,
Haul me away with winches,
Force me, without compunction,
Far from my well-loved Zoo?

Chorus—Why did the Council sell me?

Fellows of the Zoological Society called together by Mr Berkeley Hill, a surgeon, had decided to move the Court of Chancery 'To restrain the Council, their agents and servants from selling, parting with, or otherwise dealing with the elephant Jumbo, and to grant such other relief as the case may require.' The letter quoted as grounds for the action the opinion that, under its Royal Charter, the Council of the Society had no power to sell any animal, that the sale would hinder the study of zoology and thus be at variance with the objects expressed in the charter, and that it was morally wrong to sell a dangerous animal. The writer appealed for donations to a Zoological Society Defence Fund to cover the costs of the action, and he concluded, 'judging from the legal opinions already expressed, there seems little doubt that Jumbo will remain a permanent inmate of the Zoological Gardens, Regent's Park'.

Another correspondent, next day,[29] signing himself F.Z.S., was swift to suggest that, with Jumbo sold and paid for, it was 'a piece of very questionable morality . . . to attempt to take advantage of some alleged flaw in the Society's charter to attempt to interfere with his removal. Such a proceeding, especially in relation to a foreign purchaser, should, I think, be condemned by all right-minded persons.' But by the time this letter was published on the Tuesday morning Romer, counsel for the dissident Fellows, had already appeared on Monday in the High Court before Mr Justice Chitty who, after some discussion, had granted an interim injunction forbidding the removal of Jumbo before the hearing of the case was completed in the course of the next few days.

This interim injunction had been requested by Mr Berkeley Hill because he understood that passage had been booked for Jumbo on the *Egyptian Monarch* due to sail on the Thursday, and he feared that if Jumbo could be got into the crate Newman would at once take him out of the Zoo to the docks for embarkation. Mr Justice Chitty allowed himself to be informed in Court of something he was unlikely to have missed in the newspapers—Jumbo's reluctance to enter his travelling box—and then granted the temporary injunction against Jumbo's removal, with the proviso that this was not intended to prevent the defendants attempting to get him into the box. But with time so short, the injunction granted, and the final result of the case in doubt, Newman decided not to attempt to get Jumbo on board by Thursday, and so a second vessel of the Monarch Line sailed down the Thames bound for New York with an empty berth that should have accommodated the world's largest passenger.

Rally to Jumbo's defence

On the Tuesday, in the Chancery Division, the argument was pursued in greater detail. The challenge to the authority of the Council to sell any animal was difficult to sustain in the face of many examples of such transactions which had taken place in the past without any suggestion that they were in any way improper or *ultra vires*. The unique value to zoological science of Jumbo continuing to eat buns and give rides in Regent's Park had always been questionable—after all, Alice would remain as a specimen of *loxodonta africana*. The question whether the Zoo should abdicate responsibility for a potentially dangerous animal when Barnum was ready, indeed champing at the bit, to take it on, was less easy to resolve, but was a matter for a subjective rather than a legal opinion.

Mr Justice Chitty decided that the Council had a right to sell Jumbo and that the right was validly exercised. On the suggestion that the elephant might safely be retained in the Zoo he said,[30] 'If I were to accede to this argument, and afterwards the elephant should break out in a dangerous mood, and destroy human life I should be taking the management into my own hands of the Zoological Gardens, a thing which, as I say, I utterly decline to do, and it may be that the Society after the report of Mr Bartlett, would be liable to the persons injured . . . .'

The Judge commented from the Bench that he had received a number of letters, some of them from children, and that although they had not had the slightest effect upon his mind it was nevertheless extremely improper that they should have been sent. He delivered his judgment upon the motion of the dissident Fellows against the Council with finality, if not crispness: 'The result, therefore, is that upon all these grounds which I have gone through on account of the apparent importance of the case with some greater detail than I otherwise should have done, the motion fails.'

It was however a close run thing, and had Berkeley Hill and his associates taken their action earlier it would have succeeded. It was ruled that the original sale had, in law, been defective because the sub-committee which dealt with the matter contained less than the required quorum of five Fellows. Even after Barnum had paid his money the sale could have been declared invalid on these grounds and Barnum given back his two thousand pounds plus damages. But the fact that a full Council meeting had subsequently ratified the sale, before the Chancery Court action, had deprived the dissident Fellows of what would have proved to be a winning point.

Commenting upon the judgment in a fourth leader, *The Times* expanded a little upon the advisability as distinct from the legality of the sale:

> To sell Jumbo to Mr Barnum may have been safer to English visitors to the Gardens. To build a stronger stable would have been kinder to Jumbo himself . . . . The Council of the Zoological Society tell Jumbo in effect to crush and trample upon Americans if he will, but not upon us. That is a somewhat startling application of the principle of *caveat emptor*. But Mr Barnum is willing to run the risk . . . . It is well that children should crowd in thousands to the Zoological Gardens, and as a parting act of kindness, or cruelty, stuff the hero of the hour with buns innumerable. But it speaks volumes for the fundamental levity of adult nature that men have, for the last fortnight, given the first and foremost place in those of their thoughts which did not regard themselves, not to kingdoms and their destinies, but to Jumbo. It is too much to hope that we have heard the last of this famous elephant; but perhaps Jumbo's future will not monopolize conversation after Mr Justice Chitty's decision of yesterday.

But the censorious tone of *The Times* was unavailing. 'Jumbomania' had not yet reached its peak. On the day that Jumbo should have embarked in the *Egyptian Monarch* there were 4,626 visitors to the Zoo compared with 214 on the corresponding Wednesday of the previous year. The London correspondent of a provincial newspaper wrote,

Rally to Jumbo's defence

'It is difficult to make cool-headed people in the country understand or realise this ridiculous "Jumbo" craze. Yet it may be said that the breath of thousands of worthy people hung upon the decision of the Judge, and thousands of lips are now declaring the name of Chitty is synonymous with injustice, lack of humanity and patriotism. It is a ridiculous rage assuredly, yet the fervour of it can only be compared to the Jingoism of three years ago.' The *Evening Standard*, judging better than *The Times* the hysterical mood of the public—or at least its own public—had newsboys on the streets selling a special edition which carried the news of Chitty's judgment in the High Court on its front page under a banner headline 'Jumbo is to Go'.

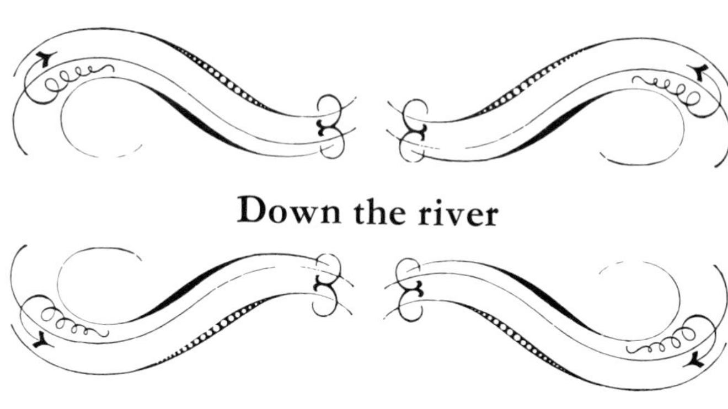

Down the river

Mr Justice Chitty's decision in the Chancery Court on 8 March removed any legal obstacle to Jumbo's departure, and the suspicion that other, less legitimate, processes might keep the elephant at Regent's Park had vanished now that Scott was cooperating so readily with Elephant Bill Newman. For the third time, a passage was booked for Jumbo and his retinue, this time in the *Assyrian Monarch* sailing for New York in the fourth week of March. But the near certainty that he would now go only increased the public interest in Jumbo. The attendance figures at the Zoo rose very sharply. Many people came with their children to have a last look at an old friend, and many more, stimulated by the publicity, came to see him for the first time before it was too late.

Week ending	Attendance
25 February	12,116
4 March	33,526
11 March	43,653
18 March	61,863

The total attendance during these four hectic weeks was more than seven times that for the corresponding period of the previous year. The money taken at the gate in the 1881 period was £444, while the figure for 1882 was £3078. Disposing of Jumbo had proved to be much more troublesome than the Council had anticipated, but much more profitable too.

Barnum offered a further thousand pounds to the Zoo authorities if they would accept responsibility for delivering Jumbo, crated, on board the ship, but Bartlett and the Council were happy enough with the bargain as originally struck. They would give every assistance with moving Jumbo, but if there should be any further delay, Newman would have the worry and the Zoo would have only the profit. It seemed, however, that there would be no more hitches, at least not with getting Jumbo into his crate. The box was dug into position like an archway—or lych-gate—outside the elephant's quarters, and on Saturday, 11 March he walked through for the first time and was at once led through again and again to reinforce his acceptance. The London correspondent of a West Country newspaper[1] reported, rather frostily, the way in which the Capital received this news:

> Jumbo has been trapped! Such was the announcement made with a groan of despair this morning by your metropolitan 'Sabbath-breaking contemporaries' as the . . . Kirk Session stigmatises the Sunday papers. It will be a relief to everyone who is not a disciple of 'Jumboism' when Jumbo is caged on board ship. It is now shrewdly suspected and gravely asserted that Jumbo's obstinacy has been simulated by his late and present masters, who have 'worked it up' for the benefit of both.

Meanwhile the crowds poured in to see Jumbo, who plainly enjoyed the extra attention and the unprecedented quantity of fruit, buns, and pastries that he was offered. When some kind-hearted visitors turned aside from the enclosure where he held court and threw a few titbits to the Indian elephant next door Jumbo thrust his huge head over the fence, joined trunks with his neighbour and wrestled with him before snatching the offerings away. Watching all this, Alice showed signs of irritation at receiving so little attention and food.

Each day, a well-dressed woman moved purposefully

among the crowds around Jumbo, distributing leaflets which had been printed at her own expense. The leaflets contained a prayer she had composed, asking God's pardon for those who had sold Jumbo, and seeking divine intervention to prevent him going to America. Three times a day she went on her knees opposite Jumbo's enclosure, personally offering up her prayer.

The interest in Jumbo's fate was not however confined to London. Hundreds of letters were received at the Zoo, and at the headquarters of the RSPCA, from all over the country and from abroad. Most of them protested at the sale, although a certain number suggested ways to overcome the difficulties of transporting Jumbo. Letters for the Secretary of the Zoological Society were addressed[2] to 'the dreadful Mr Sclater' and 'the icebound official', while he, Bartlett, and the Council were zoologically described as 'skunks', 'reptiles', 'monsters', and 'craven beasts'. Scott received his share of abuse and advice, some correspondents accusing him of being a Judas, others beseeching him to do everything to save the nation's pet, even to the point of accepting a bribe to 'do something to induce Jumbo not to go'. Some letters contained threats that violent reprisals would be taken against Zoo property, or members of the Council personally, if Jumbo were allowed to go to America. Perhaps most remarkable were the letters from adults to Jumbo himself, one from a clergyman encouraging him to 'make a firm fight of it'.

It was rather touching that thousands of buns should arrive by post from children, but other gifts sent to Jumbo were extraordinary in quantity and almost incredible in variety. Fruit, sweets, cakes, biscuits and other delicacies; a very large pumpkin which was put on one side to be a treat for him when he left; wines, spirits, beer, and twelve dozen oysters which Scott said guardedly[3] 'were put where they would do more good'. Similar diplomacy must presumably have been exercised to ensure that certain other gifts did not go to waste in the elephant house: the bouquets of expensive flowers, the cigars, the snuff, the long gold neck-chain, the loving cup. Whether Jumbo was allowed to demolish and consume the wedding cake sent to him is not revealed, nor is the actual fate of the locks of hair whose erstwhile owners must have cherished sentimental fantasies about what Jumbo might do with them.

It is difficult to see how Zoo officials could suppress a certain contemptuous irritation with people who professed to know and love an animal so well, and yet were not only ignorant of the beast's needs and fancies, but were arrogantly unaware of their own stupidity. At least the person who sent Jumbo 'corrective pills to prevent disorder during his voyage' understood the scale of the problem, if it existed at all. Sufficient pills were supplied to fill a large box two feet square.

A Superintendent of the RSPCA, on duty in the Zoo to keep an eye on the way Jumbo was crated and removed, reported that,[4] 'An elderly lady, who appeared to be quite sane, came in a cab at 6.30 a.m. on Friday last, bringing with her six pounds of hot-house grapes, about four pounds of raisins, with apples, oranges, cakes, biscuits, and sweets to eat, and wall-flowers and daffodils for Jumbo to smell. She also brought a nice basket for the elephant to feed out of. Before Jumbo had finished the delicacies, he seized the basket and ate it, ribbons and all, in preference to the grapes. The lady seemed disconcerted, and said to me, "He is rude and ungrateful." But I said, "He is quite rational for he prefers his natural food (twigs) or something like it." She asked, "Do you think he likes meat; shall I bring him a nice leg of mutton?" I said, "He is not carnivorous." She asked, "Now, what would be a treat to him, do you think?" I said, "Old birch-brooms." The lady went away quite crestfallen.'

Like any great furore which excites public interest and the attention of the Press, the Jumbo incident attracted the exhibitionist, the commercial opportunist, and the mentally disturbed. Someone sent a large night-cap for Jumbo and a widow's cap for Alice, one firm delivered a sewing-machine, and it was reported that poison had been found in a parcel of buns.

The provincial newspapers kept their readers informed

of the progress of Jumbo's affairs in London. The *Manchester Evening News*, for instance, carried news and editorial comment almost every day, while at the other end of the country, in Devonshire, the *Western Daily Mercury* did the same. This paper reported that a Plymouth shopkeeper exhibited in his window a sketch, by a local artist, depicting Jumbo with Scott brushing out his cage. The report went on,[5] 'the number of people who, at times, blocked the foot thoroughfare eager to see the "shadow" of the substance which excited newspaper editors and readers alike, justified the good offices of the pavement patrol'.

Capitalising on the excitement a London publisher[6] brought out a penny pamphlet called *Jumbo Barnum, 'Prince of Humbugs'*. This purported to be written by Barnum himself but was in fact largely made up of material from a 'ghosted' autobiography published many years before. There was a short passage about the purchase of Jumbo and the remainder was a rehash of the old book which described Barnum's colourful life, not omitting, indeed probably exaggerating, the extent to which he had on occasion fooled the public, to their amusement and his profit. He declared 'The titles of "Humbug" and "Prince of Humbugs" were first applied to me by myself. I made the title part of my stock-in-trade .... my doctrine is that a man may, by common usage, be termed a "humbug" without by any means impeaching his integrity.'

Barnum felt happy that this provocative pamphlet would help keep the British public bubbling with controversy about his part in the sale of what some were calling a national institution. He had never been inhibited about trying to snap up any British institution or monument which he believed would attract crowds to his show in America. He was aware, too, that even if such an attempted *coup* failed, it would still bring to his name the notoriety that he believed was good publicity. In the past he had almost managed to get possession of the cottage in which Shakespeare was born at Stratford, intending to dismantle it carefully and ship it to New York for re-assembly in his museum. At the last moment, however, a syndicate of horrified Englishmen managed to get their bid accepted instead, and they turned the historic building over to the Shakespeare Trust. But, as Barnum said, 'Had they slept a few days longer, I should have made a rare speculation.'[7] He almost brought off a similarly audacious *coup* when, with contracts drawn up for signature, a deal fell through at the eleventh hour and Madame Tussaud's remained in Baker Street instead of being carried off to America. Negotiations did not however proceed so far when he offered the British Government a large sum to be allowed to exhibit Cetewayo, the newly captured King of the Zulus. He received on that occasion the sort of instant and outraged refusal that he had expected from the Zoological Society when he first approached them about Jumbo.

Barnum was always prepared to act the humbug to the British people—there was even a rumour, undenied by him, that he had secretly put up money to initiate court action to prevent Jumbo's sale. But as the Jumbo controversy grew fiercer he deemed it prudent to let it be known that he might bring the elephant back to England with his show in a few months time, or even return him permanently to the Zoo after a stay in America.

Although a superficial glance at the newspapers of the day might have given the impression that all the people of England were ranged on one side against the Council of the Zoological Society on the other, there were in fact some who shouted, or at least muttered, against the sentimental storm. The Editor of *Vanity Fair*,[8] a staunch supporter of Jumbo, complained about the apathy, or perhaps the healthy realism, of the very young:

> The children of the present day appear to be inclined to take much the same views on the Jumbo question as their fathers take of other public questions. A little boy, aged four, who was taken to see the excellent elephant a few days ago, and whose sympathy it was sought to arouse by pointing out that Jumbo did not like to

leave his home, replied, very readily, 'Why not? I suppose he can get another home!' The same little boy was very much disappointed with Alice, who, he declared, 'did not look miserable at all.'

But telling the crowd what should have been obvious was not left solely to a child as it had been in the matter of the Emperor's new clothes. Mr Punch sounded a deeper note:[9]

Man and Beast

[*The Elephant Jumbo having been purchased by Mr Barnum (U.S.), a scheme has been set on foot to defray the expenses of keeping this remarkable animal on this side of the Atlantic. Funds are plentiful.*—Précis from Daily Papers.]

[*Right down East (London) exists an institution called the London Cottage Mission. Its object is to lighten (at the Mission House, 67, Salmon's Lane, Limehouse, E.C.) the sufferings of the very poor, and when funds permit, a dinner of Irish Stew is given every Wednesday, to the starving children of the East End. Funds are not plentiful.*—Précis not from the Daily Papers.]

I say, Master, d'ye hear them say of what they're
going to do—
They're going to sell the Elephant what lives up in
the Zoo;
An animal what lives on buns and cakes and things
that nice,
And for this animal they've give a most tremenjous
price.
They can sell their precious Elephant, but what I
wants to know
Is whether you think I would fetch a dollar for a show?
For I heard the people telling as how they meant to down
Sufficient 'ready' for to keep that Elephant in Town.
They say there's piteous letters from children what is
nobs,
A-wishing to plank down their coin in fivers, skivs,
and bobs;

A-crying and a-weeping 'cos of that big brute beast,
And there isn't one of them knows what a child is here down East.
We can't get the buns and sugar, and the apples and the cakes,
But we has to live as best we can, or leastways living 'fakes';
We can feel the gnawing hunger and *we* never gets our fill,
Nor columns in the TELEGRAPH when TOM or DICK falls ill.
There's no national subscription to keep us over here—
No! It strikes me they're uncommon glad when 'outward bound' we steer.
But then *we're* not all elephants, we're only rags and bone,
To be gathered by the dustman, or be left unfed, alone;
To be cast upon the gutter, and to grovel in the slums;
To seldom have a decent meal, and raven for the crumbs;
To take to lying and to theft, to blasphemy and curse,
Maybe to fill the prison cell, maybe to leave it worse.
No pretty children pray for us, no parents write with tears
In papers 'bout our destiny, our feelings and our fears;
And yet down East there's one good work—(God bless its aim, say I)—
Though this aim mayn't be too noble nor partickerlerly high—
It's to give a weekly mouthful to the little starving brats
What hasn't got the skewerfuls of meat what has the cats.
I think they're somewhat better than an elephant at ease;
I think they're somewhat better for to keep this side the seas;

And I think if these subscriptions would subscribe
for Irish stew,
They'd do a nobler work than to keep this Jumbo at
the Zoo,
Tho' they might subscribe to both, you see, and keep
their Jumbo too.

Down the river

The digging in of Jumbo's crate outside his house turned out to be a very good idea. Alice had been led into it without any difficulty, and by 15 March, over a week before he was due to leave, Jumbo was happy to walk freely through the box and had on occasion been loosely chained inside it. Some of the crowds flocking into the Gardens were almost as interested in the box as in Jumbo, and they gave it the status of an English monument by writing their names all over its sides. Among the jumble of pencilled signatures and dates were plaintive messages: 'Jumbo. don't go', 'Jumbo come back Christmas'. Only a tiny fraction of the hundreds clamouring for a place on

Out through the box

his back could be gratified, and Scott profited correspondingly. Those hoping to persuade the keeper to let their children have the next ride pushed forward, and they were pressed even closer to the ambling elephant by the thousands who had come to watch. There were far too many people present for safety. Bartlett said that he had never seen them so densely packed as they were during Jumbo's last Saturday, when nearly ten thousand people came into the Gardens, all of them wanting to look at the elephant and the scenes of excitement which surrounded him. Jumbo himself remained majestically calm, except on one occasion when a sudden shower of rain caused a bursting open of umbrellas all round him and for a moment it looked as though he might take fright and trample on people who were already almost under his feet. But Scott had him quiet again in a second or two, and only a few of those watching realised in one alarming moment just what Bartlett feared might occur if an elephant ran amok in the crowded grounds.

On Monday, 20 March an almost incredible eighteen and a half thousand people came into the Zoological Gardens. *The Times*[10] wrote 'It is unlikely that Jumbo will again walk in the Gardens. His last riders in London were probably those who bestrode his broad back on Monday, much to their own gratification and the amusement of the large number of spectators assembled.' On the Tuesday Jumbo did not go out in the Gardens but remained in his house with his forefeet loosely chained to the rails. He stayed like this until he was given his breakfast at seven o'clock on the Wednesday morning.

At eight o'clock, with Jumbo replete, and it was hoped in good humour, the work began to get him crated and pulled out of the Zoo on the trolley. It was estimated that the total weight of crate and contents would be about twelve tons, and, even ignoring the almost unimaginable chaos which might result if Jumbo decided to be really intractable, it was a complex problem to get such a huge load through London to the docks and onto the boat for America. Route and time had to be chosen to avoid sharp bends and narrow entrances, and traffic. The operation was further complicated by the fact that only certain cranes within the Thames docks were strong enough to lift the load, and that its transfer from land to water could only take place at favourable states of the tide. The plan was to take Jumbo by road to the nearest convenient dock to the Zoo—St Katharine Dock—where he was to be loaded onto a barge and towed a few miles down-river to the Millwall Docks where he would be transferred to the *Assyrian Monarch*. The whole journey might take several days, and humanity—not to say prudence—required that at all stages Jumbo should be fed, watered, and otherwise comforted, and that he should not be roughly handled nor left in any place where noise or other disturbance might frighten or annoy him.

Down the river

Before it was fully light on what was to be a very long day for Newman and Scott, they set to work to get the elephant harnessed up in the chains to which he had become reasonably accustomed over the previous few weeks. The

Secured at last

hobbles on his legs were raised higher, and the other chains placed round his head and body, leaving his mouth and trunk free, but restricting any violent movement of his head so that he would be unable to put his full strength into delivering a blow with his tusks or trunk.

Outside the elephant house, the morning was crisp and cold. The night frost had thickly coated the roof and sides of the wooden crate, and the iron straps which strengthened it were wet and black and shining.

Just after nine o'clock the Zoo's heavy gang was summoned. These were the labourers, carpenters, and blacksmiths whose job was to close and strengthen the crate once Jumbo was inside; to dig out the trolley; and to provide a reserve of strength to be used to help the horses at critical moments when they were pulling the trolley up the inclined end of the trench and then along the paths to the gates of the Gardens. The frost was brushed off the crate, and water which had dripped down inside was mopped up.

Jumbo had shown some signs of disquiet when he was chained, jerking his legs and kneeling from time to time, but he went willingly when Scott led him out of the house. He stepped into the box, as he was now accustomed, expecting to pass through it for his usual outing in the grounds. When he was inside, Scott called, 'Whoa, Jumbo' and, obedient and unsuspecting, the elephant at once stopped. In a flash Newman and Scott secured the chains on his forelegs round iron bars on the side of the box, and Jumbo was trapped. He could not at first understand this unexpected delay in getting out for his walk in the Gardens, and when he felt his legs to be immobilised he stretched out his trunk in an enquiring way towards Scott. Then, realising he was caught, he knelt, putting his forehead on the ground in the plaintive attitude of submission which Bartlett said was commonly adopted by elephants when they recognised that they had been overcome by superior force.

The next step was to get Jumbo's back legs secured to the inside of the box, and this proved to be a frustrating task which took longer than two hours. Time and again Jumbo managed to avoid the loops of heavy, leather-covered chain which were to encircle each back leg. Sometimes he stood immobile with his foot on the chain, then, after seemingly endless coaxing until the loop was almost in place, he would kick it to one side and they had to start all over again. When a dozen of the labourers tried to lift his foot by hauling on a heavy rope, passed over a branch of a tree and attached to one of his hind legs, Jumbo gave an impressive demonstration of his strength by snapping a manila hawser several inches thick with one almost casual flick of the leg.

It was nearly midday before he was finally chained by all four legs in the crate, and during the operation he had reared and kicked, and plunged and knelt, and looked at times as though he was trying to turn a somersault out of the box. When his back legs were both secured he struggled furiously for five minutes or so, swaying his whole weight against the sides of the crate and digging into it ferociously with the broken stumps of his tusks so that pieces of wood and a few chips of ivory flew in all directions.

Since early morning the public had been allowed into the Gardens in the ordinary way and there was a large crowd of spectators around the elephant enclosure. Many of them felt that Jumbo must surely smash up the box and free himself, but after his five minutes of particularly violent struggling when his hind feet had first been secured, he suddenly became quiet and even put out his trunk to Scott and accepted a few titbits. The chains were then slowly drawn tighter, with very little opposition from Jumbo, until he stood in the open box with each foot able only to move about fifteen inches. During his struggles he had scraped a raw place on his tail by rubbing against one of the iron bars, which was quickly wrapped in sacking to prevent it causing further injury.

The carpenters and blacksmiths were now called upon to close the ends of the cage, and to strengthen it with thick wooden planks and iron bars which had already been cut to size and were ready to be slid into clamps on the crate and bolted in place. The workmen placed all their materials and tools near the box ready to start work, and a murmur of amusement and pleasure rose from the crowd as Jumbo's trunk snaked out and began delicately to examine the various items laid on the ground within his reach. The work was much impeded by Jumbo, who tried hard to push aside each plank as soon as it was slipped into place and before it could be secured with bolts. Every time he succeeded in knocking out a plank—and he did so many times—the crowd gave him a cheer. Warming to the contest, he began to throw himself about violently and to shake the crate so that men working on the top frequently jumped off in alarm. It was intended that the upper half of one end of the crate should be closed with swing doors like a stable, but just when the last screw had been put in place Jumbo demonstrated that anything light enough to swing on hinges was too flimsy to withstand the attentions of an angry elephant. The doors were smashed into jagged fragments in seconds and the crowd gave a roar of mingled alarm and congratulation. The wreckage was removed and replaced by stout planks through which Jumbo could clearly be seen and which were far enough apart for him to be able to extend his

Inspecting and inscribing the crate

Jumbo impedes the carpenters

trunk. By the time all this was accomplished and the earth dug out of the trench it was well into the afternoon before six great draught horses could be hitched onto the trolley by Pickford's men and a start made to haul it up to ground level with its huge load.

It was a sharp slope up from the bottom of the trench, which had been dug so that Jumbo would not have to walk up a ramp into the crate. But the trolley ran tolerably well on the iron rails in the trench, and each time the horses gained a couple of inches heavy baulks of timber were put behind the wheels so that they could not run back. Jumbo gave remarkably little trouble as the horses heaved the trolley out of the trench, and within three quarters of an hour his crate was standing on ground level.

The journey through the Gardens to the gates of the Zoo went less smoothly. The engineers consulted by the Council had declared that the wheels of the trolley were too narrow to carry such a heavy load, especially on the soft paths within the grounds. But although the Council's action in seeking professional advice might have helped them in Court if they had been sued after a possible accident, it could scarcely have been expected to have any practical influence on the way in which Jumbo was removed—indeed it might not have been sought for that purpose since the responsibility for moving the elephant rested with Barnum's men. The plans had been made, and the trolley built and dug into the trench, before the report was called for. It was completed and delivered to the Zoo less than twenty-four hours before Jumbo was fastened in the crate for removal. Almost as soon as the horses started to pull the trolley out of Jumbo's enclosure towards the gates it was apparent that the consultant engineers' criticism of the wheels had been sound.

Immediately outside the enclosure the horses had to negotiate a sharp turn, with the path only just a little wider than the trolley and its load. An additional hazard was the fact that for some distance the path was only separated by a low grassy mound from the edge of a bank sloping steeply down to the Regent's Park Canal. To make a difficult situation worse, the gravel path was particularly soft there. The police and the Zoo foremen were keeping spectators out of the way, but just as this awkward place was being negotiated, *The Times* reported,[11] 'some mischievous person in the crowd shouted "Whoa", and the horses stopped'. Before the team could be got moving again, the wheels of the trolley began to sink into the ground and soon the axles were buried. The workmen slaved away, digging, jacking, and levering planks under the wheels. By the time the trolley was out of the hole and moving forward again it was nearly 7 p.m. The crowds had been moved out of the Gardens and darkness had fallen. With many halts, the work continued by lamp-light on an unpleasant wintry night with a cold wind and flurries of snow. By 10 p.m. the trolley had been dragged about a hundred yards, leaving deep ruts in the path behind it. But the last of the serious obstacles had been passed, a pair of trees with a gap between them that looked to some as though it would prove too narrow. The horses were taken off, tarpaulins fixed over the ends of the crate to protect Jumbo from the wind, and most of the men, including Scott, went off to get a rest and some supper.

Two men came and nailed onto the crate a wooden board reading, 'Barnum, Bailey and Hutchinson, New York, U.S.A.' Presumably this was intended more for advertisement than because there was any fear that the crate might miscarry to the wrong address. Whether it was due to the fixing of this board, or because he had been left alone in strange circumstances, Jumbo began to show signs of disquiet.

At about 10.15 p.m. he started to move about inside the crate as far as he was able, and to stretch out his trunk and play peevishly with straw lying on the little platform at the front of the trolley. When one of the men came forward with a nose-bag containing some chaff left from the horses' feed, Jumbo snatched up the bag and threw it at him. Then gradually he became more and more violent, throwing himself about in such a frenzy that he gashed his forehead but did not appear to notice it. The trolley began to rock to and fro on its wheels and but for the chocks under them would have rolled further. The crate had prudently been left shored up with heavy props otherwise Jumbo might well have turned it on its side. He was at his most violent just before eleven o'clock, trumpeting, blowing blasts of steamy breath from his trunk into the frosty lamplight, and smashing against the sides of his great box so furiously that frightened onlookers were certain that it was only a matter of time before it was in pieces. Fortunately Scott, who had been urgently summoned from his supper, came hurrying back and as soon as Jumbo heard his voice he began to calm down until at last he was quiet again and would take food from his keepers. It was nevertheless after midnight before the horses—ten of them, harnessed two abreast—could be put between the shafts attached to the trolley. Once more the wheels had sunk into the ground, but in less than an hour the workmen and the horses together had got Jumbo moving forward again.

What one paper called 'a rough crowd' had gathered outside the gates of the Zoo in spite of the late hour and unpleasant weather. They passed the time with some raucous singing in which 'Rule Britannia' figured prominently, and at about one in the morning they at last saw the great team of horses and Jumbo's crate slowly approach the gates. But, as it came through, the trolley struck the bank on one side and stopped. The front wheels sank into the soft ground and the crowd cheered and clapped, and shouted that the Yankees should not have Jumbo. But their jubilant hopes of seeing Jumbo once more walk back through the gates soon faded. The workmen quickly jacked up the trolley, with an expertise acquired from much practice over the previous ten hours, and at half past one Jumbo's trolley was safely out onto the firm road outside the Zoo and moving off quite briskly towards the Docks.

The crowd followed, most of them on foot, but with a few reporters and one or two 'bloods' occupying half a dozen hansoms. It was a noisy, somewhat bibulous mob, probably never above two hundred, but they were good-tempered enough and caused little trouble to the constables who, under their Superintendent, had been on duty in the Zoo and were now deployed along the route to the Docks, being warned by electric telegraph when to take up their positions.

It was just before two a.m. when the procession came out of Regent's Park through the Gloucester Gate. As the trolley passed through the gate it scraped the ironwork and stopped, but the delay was brief and when they started again Jumbo trumpeted and the crowd cheered. The route was through Albany Street to King's Cross, past Clerkenwell Prison, and along Commercial Street to Tower Hill and the entrance to the Docks. Detours were made to avoid difficult gradients, and progress should have been swift behind Pickford's team of powerful horses. But the trolley wheels which had sunk into the ground when they were standing still now proved equally unsuited to rapid revolution. The wooden wheels and axles were frequently seen to be smoking, and once or twice sparks glowing in the darkness suggested that they might burst into flames and give the crowd further excitement. Progress was halted more often to cool the wheels and pour water over them than to refresh the horses.

As the procession was heard approaching the sleeping streets people got up and came to their bedroom windows to catch a glimpse of a piece of comic history passing below. At the barracks in Albany Street the guard was turned out in honour of Jumbo, who took little notice. He behaved well on the journey, only showing signs of disturbance when the trolley was going downhill and he felt himself slipping forward. But Scott and Newman, riding on the platform at the front of the trolley, were able to comfort and control him. At one time he stretched his trunk out between the open planks at the front and, until dissuaded, took hold of one of the horse traces, to the delight of the crowd, who declared that Jumbo was driving himself.

It was five o'clock, with daylight dimming the street-lamps, when they arrived at the entrance to St Katharine

Dock. The sharp turn through the narrow gateway was a severe test of driving skill with such a long team of horses and a large and heavy load on a particularly unmanoeuvrable trolley. The crowd was treated to an hour of whip-cracking and harness jingling, heaving and backing, and the clatter and slip of horse-shoes on cobbles, before the trolley rattled away into the Docks, leaving those who loved Jumbo, and those who enjoyed a sensation, gathered at the gates like the group outside a prison on the morning of an execution. Soon the horses came walking back, relieved of their load, and word passed that Jumbo's crate now stood under a crane on the dockside and that his last moments on English soil were approaching.

Down the river

Moored against the wall below Jumbo was the barge *Clarence*, capable of carrying sixty tons of cargo and now ballasted with twenty-five tons of iron rails to keep her low in the water and minimise rolling if the elephant should throw his weight about when he was afloat. The many delays in the journey from the Zoo meant that they had missed the morning tide, but it was decided to get Jumbo into the barge without delay and let him rest there until midday when there would again be sufficient water to work the *Clarence* out through the locks into the Thames. The slingers put ropes round the crate, and just before seven o'clock the crane lifted it carefully a foot or two off the ground to test the positioning of the ropes. The strange

Jumbo 'drives himself'

Night drive through the streets

A rest on the way

Into the docks

sensation of feeling himself swaying very gently, and apparently unsupported below, caused Jumbo to move about vigorously, but he was quickly comforted by Scott when the crate was set down on the ground again for minor readjustments. Then, with a long grey trunk waving out through the bars, the crate was quickly lifted into the air, swung out over the edge of the wall, and lowered gently into position in the barge. Timber baulks were knocked into place between the crate and the sides of the hold to prevent movement, and then Jumbo was settled down and given a good breakfast.

Down the river

That evening the *Western Daily Mercury*'s unsympathetic London correspondent reported,[12]

> Very early this morning advanced editions of the evening papers vied with extra second editions of the morning journals in recording the pathetic fact 'Jumbo's afloat'. Many incidents are recorded tonight of the removal of the unwieldy idol. One I will narrate that has escaped the industrious chiffonniers* of Jumbo gossip. Early this morning a lady arrived at Regent's Park to witness the removal of the elephant. She had, however, come too late. Her friend—everybody's friend—was already nearing the docks. Not to be disappointed, however, she walked on foot from the Zoological Gardens to St Katharine Docks and craved admission, which was refused by the dock gate-keepers. The fair visitor turned upon a susceptible policeman a plaintive appeal, and was rewarded. Making her way to the elephant, she opened her basket, and taking two quart bottles of beer emptied them into the omnivorous trunk. Jumbo, like Falstaff, probably cried out against 'this intolerable deal of sack', but he was speedily supplied with buns and cakes from the same receptacle.

Jumbo certainly did not cry out against being given ale, to which he had long been accustomed by Scott, and indeed on this occasion he followed it with a 'chaser' of whisky and water which he showed every sign of enjoying.

* rag pickers

Hold tight

Down the river

At noon the barge was moved away from the dockside and taken out towards the river. By this time word had spread of Jumbo's presence and his imminent departure, and every vantage point was occupied by those who had business in the Docks, and by many others who had on one pretext or another gained admittance. The windows of offices and warehouses; roofs, walls, and bridges; even the yards of ships in dock; every possible place became a grandstand. When the tug, with the *Clarence* in tow, got out of St Katharine Dock into the open river it was greeted by an armada of small boats filled with cheering spectators, and many more lined the bank to give Jumbo a send-off as he went down-river to Millwall with the British ensign fluttering from the tug and the Stars and Stripes flying from the stern of the barge. At Millwall, an hour or so later, there were more sightseers and the tug had to thread its way through another flotilla of rowing boats, one of which—with the paint still wet—was prominently named *Jumbo*. Once out of the river and into the Millwall Dock, the barge was moored under the very powerful set of shear legs, and Jumbo's crate was lifted out of the barge onto the quay at half past three in the afternoon. During the lifting, which took less than ten minutes, it was possible to weigh the crate and contents. The total weight was twelve and a half tons, and since the box was known to be six and a half tons, it meant that Jumbo scaled six tons. He was left in his crate on the quay overnight with either Scott or Newman in attendance all the time. Next morning the *Assyrian Monarch*, which was berthed nearby, was worked in alongside the barge, and Jumbo, in his crate, was hoisted up by the shear legs and swung high in the air before being lowered into the steamer's hold.

Extensive preparations had been made to accommodate Jumbo aboard the *Assyrian Monarch*. This vessel, with a crew of ninety, normally carried about six hundred passengers. With others of her line she took many emigrants to the United States, most of them Russian Jews. This prompted a question to the Secretary of the Board of

Trade in the House of Commons about the safety of Jumbo's fellow emigrants.[13] Mr Evelyn Ashley replied that the Board of Trade could claim no control over the elephant's uncertain temper, but went on 'surveyors of the Board have been instructed to be present at the embarkation of the animal, and to take every care that no danger to the ship or passengers results from its presence on board. They are specially charged to see that the cage in which the animal is placed, is sufficiently strong to prevent it getting adrift; and, above all, that the elephant shall not be able to step on to the light awning deck from his own cage.

Farewell from the dockside

They have further been instructed to take care that the presence of the animal does not interfere with the ventilation of the ship, and the health, comfort, or safety of the passengers'.

The crate was placed in the main forward hold, resting on the third deck and with its top just projecting above the main deck, but not so far as to prevent the securing of the hatch covers if severe weather made this necessary. It was firmly wedged against the ship's structure so that it would not shift, and Jumbo's quarters were boarded off from the rest of the ship with heavy planks, and the bottom of his apartment was lined with lead to prevent any drainage into cabins below. For Jumbo's own personal comfort and sustenance there had been taken on board sixty-five trusses of hay, thirty bags of ship's biscuit, three sacks of oats and three of bran, fifty large white loaves, and two sacks of onions—his special treat. The cost of Jumbo's rations for the fortnight's voyage was estimated at twenty pounds.

By the time he was aboard, Jumbo was found to have a second cut on his forehead which was bleeding, but not apparently troubling him. Bartlett and officials of the RSPCA who had watched every stage of the removal were satisfied with all the arrangements. But, even if they had not been satisfied, informed legal opinion[14] was that they would have had no case to bring, because elephants were not specifically mentioned by the relevant Act, nor were they domestic animals within its meaning.

With Jumbo safely embarked there was a formal luncheon in the ship's dining-room. Among those present were the Sheriff of the City of London, who apologised for the absence of the Lord Mayor, and the US Consul General, who regretted that the lack of a United States Mercantile Marine compelled Jumbo to travel in a British ship. Bartlett's speech gave a biographical sketch of the principal object of the celebration, who was lunching separately below, and a member of the Zoological Society presented Newman with a gold medal. On one side was the figure of an elephant and his master, while on the obverse was inscribed 'Presented to William Newman as a token of respect and esteem by a few English friends. Frederick Trotman, Treasurer'. Mr Trotman explained that it had been purchased with a fund raised by officers and a few Fellows of the Society, no doubt as a mild snub to the dissident membership who had so vigorously opposed the sale and questioned the actions and authority of the Council.

The *Assyrian Monarch* remained at Millwall overnight on the Friday, having taken on board some eighty emigrants who had been allowed by the shipping company to join early so as to avoid travelling by rail on their Sabbath. At five o'clock on Saturday morning, assisted by two tugs, she left the Dock and proceeded down-river to Gravesend where she was to pick up several hundred more emigrants whose passage had been arranged by a representative of the Russian Jewish Fund. As the vessel passed the nautical training ships moored in the Thames the boy seamen manned the yards in Jumbo's honour: a perilous form of salute normally reserved for royalty.

The ship arrived at Gravesend at 8.30 a.m. and took on the remainder of her passengers. She was dressed overall with flags and bunting ready to welcome a distinguished party who were travelling down from London with the Baroness Burdett Coutts on the midday train from Fenchurch Street. The visitors included Lord and Lady Tenterden, a Member of Parliament, an Admiral, a General, and representatives of the Monarch Line. The Baroness was presented with a sweet-smelling bouquet of violets on behalf of the owners, and then went with her party to visit Jumbo between decks. She gave him a bun or two, wished him goodbye, and shook hands with Scott and Newman, expressing confidence that the elephant would prosper in the United States. Afterwards she inspected the emigrants' quarters, spoke to them through a Russian interpreter, and gave money for sweets and small gifts for the women and children. As she left 'the Jews pressed forward to kiss the hem of her garment, and they cheered'.[15]

Alerted by the Parliamentary question, the Board of

Trade inspectors examined the *Assyrian Monarch* with great care to ensure that the emigrants were in no possible danger from Jumbo. They ordered that no passengers were to be accommodated on the forward decks near the elephant's compartment, and consequently Barnum had to pay not only Jumbo's fare but that of the two hundred steerage passengers he displaced. In fact the final inspection at Gravesend was so extended that the pilot decided that he could not take the vessel out through the narrow channel in darkness with the strong prevailing wind. She lay off the Nore overnight and sailed early on the Sunday morning into a gale, a whole bottle of whisky being poured into Jumbo's trunk in celebration.

Down the river

The motion of the ship as she felt the waves did not trouble Jumbo. He trumpeted a little, but was well enough behaved for it to be decided that the chains round his head and body could be removed, leaving them only on his feet. This was a difficult and potentially dangerous

Jumbo's sea quarters

job for Scott, who had to squeeze into the cage between Jumbo's head and chest to get at the martingale. He took the precaution of knocking out one plank at the back of the crate and clearing away the straw to make escape easier should Jumbo prove ill-disposed. The crowd of passengers watching the proceedings did not appreciate the danger, and they laughed as Scott grovelled about under the huge animal. Newman called sharply for silence, and Scott was able to complete the job safely and Jumbo, now much freer, could put out his trunk to the people on the upper deck and receive gifts of oranges, biscuits and sweets.

On the Sunday afternoon the *Assyrian Monarch* hove to off Dover to drop the pilot. A second boat went out through the heavy seas with the pilot cutter and brought off Bartlett, Barnum's agent Davis, and a senior official of the RSPCA, all of whom had stayed aboard until the last possible moment. Returning to shore, their lives were for a few minutes in peril as waves whipped up by the gale almost swamped the small boat. When they landed, shaken and soaked, they were at once surrounded by a waiting crowd who wanted to hear the very latest news of Jumbo, now disappearing into the grey wind-blown drizzle on the way to New York.

Assyrian Monarch *dressed overall*

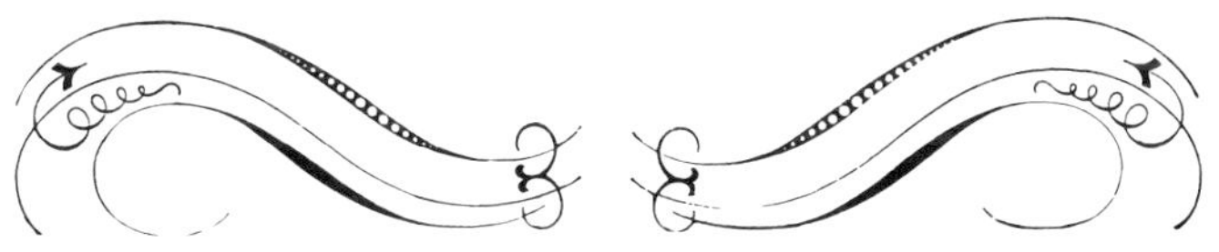

Over the sea to Broadway

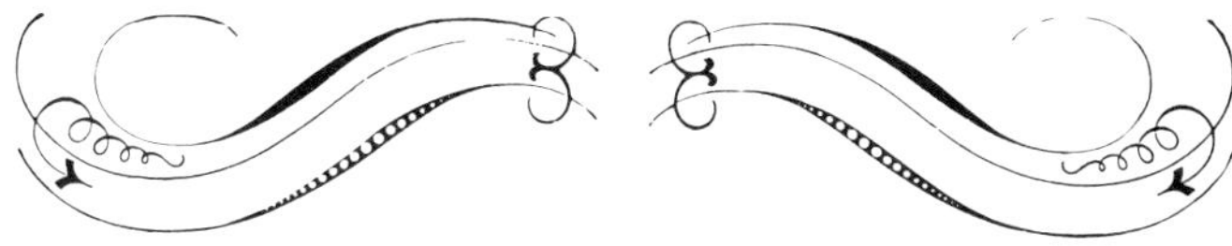

As Jumbo sailed into the distance like a passing thunderstorm, last items of news about him flashed back to London, the dying murmurs of Jumbomania persisted, and the Zoological Society occupied itself in cleaning up the mess which the controversy had made of relations between the Council and the two factions in the membership. As always, provincial papers were ready to report metropolitan follies. One[1] drew attention to the severe gales sweeping the country when the *Assyrian Monarch* sailed, and commented 'It is needless to say that the condition of Jumbo during the storm is exciting the commiseration of the votaries of Jumboism.' Another[2] reported that congregations in 'fashionable London churches were singing "for those in peril on the sea."'. On the afternoon of Monday, 27 March 1882 the signal station on the Lizard in south Cornwall reported sighting the *Assyrian Monarch* and receiving a semaphore message that Jumbo was 'well, very quiet, and unchained'. There was no further word of Jumbo's progress until he had crossed the Atlantic, although Barnum, hoping for more publicity, had arranged that reports should be thrown overboard in bouyant rubber bags. It was, however, long after the voyage was over that the first of them was washed up on the extreme south-western tip of Ireland.

During the crossing Jumbo had, on the whole, behaved well. He had Scott and Newman to look after him, assisted by nine sweepers and cleaners, and he was much pampered by passengers and crew, who gave him fruit and other delicacies, and delighted to indulge his liking for alcohol. The Chief Officer remarked[3] that Jumbo was never stinted in his supply of liquor and if he did condescend to drink water he took in ten or fifteen gallons at a time. He was sea-sick once, and for a couple of days he trumpeted more than usual, but this early nervousness soon disappeared and he settled down well to life afloat—except if he was left alone for any length of time. In the London Zoo it had been noticed that Jumbo's violent fits always subsided as soon as he was taken out of his solitary stable to walk among the people in the Gardens. Now in the strange ship-board surroundings he was happy enough during the day when there were people about, feeding him and petting him, but at night, if Scott and Newman both left him, he would become restive, and if one of them did not soon return to keep him company he would become violent and attack his cage with such fury that the crashes and thuds would echo round the ship. He smashed several of the heavy timber planks of the crate during these demonstrations, but usually he stood quietly in his box at night, sleeping on his feet for a couple of hours at a time with his trunk curled up around a beam at the front.

It was little hardship to Jumbo to have insufficient room to lie down. A modern elephant keeper of great experience[4] recalls taking a pair of elephants by sea from London to Russia. One of them was crated much as Jumbo was, but the other, tethered more freely in a shelter on deck, made little or no use of the opportunity to lie down.

One piece of apparently gratuitous mischief was reported of Jumbo during the voyage. A member of the crew was washing his laundry in a pail within reach of the crate and when Jumbo stretched out his trunk the sailor gave it what was intended to be a friendly smack. But Jumbo apparently took offence. He waited until the man had finished the job and then reached out and picked up the clean clothes, took them into the box, rolled them in the dirt on the floor until they were filthy, and then threw them back outside.

Over the sea to Broadway

Barnum had made sure that the American public was kept fully informed of the detailed symptoms of Jumbo-mania and the extent of its feverish spread among the population of England. Now, the seventy-year-old impressario of the bizarre was impatient to take delivery of his purchase so that he might personally control the

JUDY'S COMICAL PENN'ORTH

No. 12. MARCH 27th, 1882.

JUMBO'S VOYAGE

ACROSS THE ATLANTIC,

AND HIS GREAT DOINGS AMONG THE AMERICANS.

FULLY ILLUSTRATED.

"JUDY" OFFICE, 99 SHOE LANE, FLEET STREET, E.C.

Jumbo publicity and promotion which he hoped would bring crowds flocking to the circus and so confirm that his sense of business and showmanship was as acute as ever.

At day-break on 10 April 1882 the *Assyrian Monarch* lay off-shore in New York's North River, and at a very early hour she was approached by a tug carrying Barnum, Bailey, and Hutchinson of the eponymous Circus, and representatives of the Press. As soon as the two vessels were within earshot the Captain of the *Assyrian Monarch* leaned over the rail to shout to Barnum the reassurance that 'Jumbo is all right; fine as silk.' Once aboard, the party quickly gathered round Jumbo's cage to see at last the object of all the fuss, and to question Scott and Newman and the ship's officers about the voyage. One detail which particularly intrigued the reporters was Jumbo's taste for alcohol, and the fact that he frequently drank beer and had often enjoyed the special treat of a bottle of whisky during the crossing.

Jumbo was not unique among elephants as a tippler. Those in captivity were given strong drink for medicinal purposes and, in days of coarser feelings and cheaper liquor, elephants in zoos and circuses were often encouraged to take a drink in public for the amusement of spectators. The wine-bibbing elephant at Versailles in the seventeenth century had been a favourite of the Paris public. In the wild, too, elephants are apparently aware of the uses of alcohol. A modern writer[5] says, 'Many African hunters in our own time told of the elephant's fondness for strong drink. The animals have a passion for the fruit of a certain African tree, which is intoxicating when over-ripe. After eating it they become quite tipsy. Some stagger about, play silly tricks and make the forest resound with their trumpeting, others become fighting drunk and stage awkward battles.' Barnum himself exploited the peculiar satisfaction it gave audiences to see the monstrous creature caricature one of the most common and most ridiculed of human weaknesses. In one of his circus acts an elephant walked into the ring on his hind legs and sat down at a table with his trainer. He picked up a bell in his trunk and rang for a waiter, who brought a tray with food, a bottle of coloured water, and two glasses. Elephant and trainer then did a typical clown routine. When the man looked away at the audience the elephant seized the bottle in his trunk and emptied it into his mouth. The waiter was recalled with another bottle and the performance repeated several times until finally the elephant slumped on his seat, cooling himself with a fan waved in his trunk, before getting up from the table and staggering drunkenly around and out of the ring to a tumult of laughter and applause.

Barnum was well known to be an advocate of Temperance, and when the party gathered on *Assyrian Monarch* was told of Jumbo's drinking habits he gave a convincing display of surprise. He was apparently particularly startled, and a little put out, that the elephant had been given whisky. The chief officer assured him that Jumbo thoroughly enjoyed a bottle of Scotch and offered to fetch one for a demonstration. Barnum dissented, but generously gave way when everyone else, particularly the reporters, clamoured to be allowed to see the trick. As the bottle was being unwrapped and the stopper removed, the beneficiary's eager attention was obvious to all. Jumbo stretched out his trunk with the end curled up like the bell of a saxophone and, after the contents of the bottle had been tipped into this moist thick-walled receptacle, he transported it to his mouth without spillage. When the last drop had been drunk, he gave a deep sigh and waved his trunk hopefully towards the delighted spectators. Barnum's last word on the subject was to the effect that Jumbo would have been a real monster if only Scott had not stunted his growth with alcohol.

It had been planned to remove Jumbo in his crate to the shore as soon as possible, using a large floating steam derrick—a combined crane and barge. But there was a hold-up in these arrangements when it was found that the engineer was not on board the derrick, and that without him steam could not be raised. While the missing man was being sought, and his craft brought to readiness, Barnum

THE PARTING.

Farewell, farewell, poor JUMBO cried, farewell sweet ALICE, my dear bride,
And to you all in London City, with woe I sing my parting ditty;
For now I'm caged and soon will be an exile o'er the foaming sea.

THE ROUTE TO MILLWALL.

Now through streets I slowly go, while my poor heart is full of woe,
And to each child I see in grief I fondly wave my handkerchief,
And weep that I shall see no more their rosy cheeks on Albion's shore

and his party were given lunch on board the *Assyrian Monarch*, and Jumbo was given a peck of apples they had brought with them.

During lunch Barnum was able to tell the reporters more about the cost of Jumbo, which he estimated to be about thirty thousand dollars. One third of this was the price

GETTING ON BOARD.
Next in my cage from Millwall Quay they swung me up without delay,
And when within the vessel's hold I felt the pain of being sold,
Without a face or form near that I was wont to love so dear.

THE VOYAGE.
They cared for me well going out to sea, but could not soothe my misery,
For naught could banish from my mind the wife and friends I left behind,
And oh! to crown my sorrows quick the waves arose and made me sick

paid to the London Zoological Society and the remainder was spent on all the varied expenses of transport from Regent's Park to New York, including the two cancelled passages. Barnum revealed that the amount of duty to be paid was still under discussion with the Customs authorities. He claimed that Jumbo had been purchased primarily for breeding purposes, not for show, and should therefore be duty-free. The arguments had yet to be resolved, but meanwhile the Customs House had agreed that Jumbo might be landed under bond.

It was nearly half-past four in the afternoon before the steam derrick arrived alongside and the last stage of Jumbo's journey began. By half-past five the hatch covers had been cleared away, ropes and chains fixed around the crate, and the hundreds of people in small boats, or gathered on the shore nearby, prepared to catch their first glimpse of the famous immigrant. Jumbo himself, sensing that his life was about to be disrupted yet again, began to sway to and fro in an ominous manner. He was given a bottle of whisky by Scott, then a large quantity of biscuit, and this quietened him. With Scott riding on the little platform at the front, and with Jumbo's trunk waving through the bars, the crate was smoothly lifted high in the air out of the steamer's hold and dropped gently onto the deck of the derrick. To the cheers of the crowd it puffed away from the side of the *Assyrian Monarch* towards the Battery, where a crowd of nearly two thousand waited to greet Jumbo's arrival on American soil. He was quite calm on the short trip, trumpeting once or twice in apparent answer to the welcoming whistles of tugs and other vessels, and only showing signs of serious disturbance when Scott went away from the front of the crate for a few moments to speak to someone on board about the landing arrangements.

When Jumbo's crate was lifted onto the quay and placed on its trolley the same difficulties arose as had done in London. It seemed at one stage that the combined efforts of sixteen horses, and the help of several hundred men from the crowd pulling on a long rope, would not get the trolley out of some soft ground and onto the roadway. When no progress had been made after several hours the crowd got more and more impatient at standing in the cold on a miserable, wet night. They shouted for Jumbo to be led out of his crate and walked to the Garden, but Barnum and his colleagues did not dare take the risk that the elephant might run amok with disastrous results to himself and the public. A message was sent back to Madison Square ordering a couple of elephants to be sent down to the pier to assist. But before the arrival of Gipsy and Chief, two circus elephants well used to street parades, the horses had got the trolley out onto the hard road and it moved along fairly well, away from the river towards State Street.

There was a delay while the height of the crate was measured and thankfully found to be two inches less than the height of the elevated railway track. Then a start was made again with only eight horses pulling the trolley. Gipsy and Chief followed with their trainer, after them came the other eight horses, and finally a jostling crowd, now reduced to a hundred or so, all getting soaked in the pouring rain.

There were a number of brief stops to cool the axles with buckets of water scooped up from the gutters. At one point the trolley got stuck in loose earth thrown up from road works and Gipsy and Chief were required to help the horses by pushing with their heads against the back of the crate. The strange procession passed up Broadway at about midnight and reached Madison Square Garden some time after one o'clock, with no other untoward incident than a frightened cab horse running away, and a few trumpets from Jumbo.

When they arrived at the Garden it was discovered that the crate was too big to pass through the entrance, so it was decided that Jumbo should spend the remainder of the night outside, with Scott and Newman in close attendance, and with tarpaulins thrown over his box to protect him from the weather and the stares of passers-by. He would be moved in to join the other twenty-odd elephants in the morning.

Jumbo's disembarkation was reported in the morning newspapers which also carried a large advertisement from Barnum:

That Colossus of Elephants now here

JUMBO

The biggest and most famous animal in the world.
The people of two hemispheres excited over his purchase.

Just arrived from the Royal Zoological Gardens, London.

Costing nearly $30,000

The mighty monarch of beasts landed amid the
Enthusiastic shouts of half a million people.

All England against his departure.
All America bound to have him.

Brought here against the 'regrets' of Victoria
The Prince of Wales, and despite of injunctions, the law.

Ridden upon by the Queen, Royal Family, and over a million children.

Its loss mourned by every child in Great Britain
Now on exhibition every afternoon and evening.

The *New York Times* referred in its leader that day to the arrival of Jumbo and to Barnum's advertisement:

It would, of course, have been very absurd for the English nation to take the ground that the Zoological Society had no right to sell its own elephant to an American showman; but as we have already taken the equally absurd ground that a French society has no right to dig a canal in Columbia,* we need not bear too hardly upon English absurdities. However, in spite of the outcries of the British press, Mr Barnum has triumphed, and it is no wonder that he has broken out

* In 1903 Panama seceded from Columbia and signed a treaty with the United States for the building of the Canal.

> into a wild and eloquent song of victory, thinly disguised as an advertisement . . . .

Commenting on the reference to the Queen riding Jumbo, the leader continued,

> Imposing as this statement is, it is also characterized by a wonderful self-restraint on the part of the writer. He does not mention, except in the most general way, the nature of the Queen's intimacy with Jumbo. Now it is well known in Court circles that from her earliest years her Majesty has been enthusiastically attached to Jumbo. There was a time when she was accustomed to keep Jumbo in the Windsor Castle Park, where she would often romp with him by the hour, making him fetch and carry like a dog and rolling with him in innocent delight upon the turf. Later in her life, when the danger that her Majesty might by accident roll upon Jumbo and seriously injure him became too obvious to be disregarded, the Queen ceased to romp with him, though she still kept up the custom of having him sit by her side at the tea-table and 'beg' for lumps of sugar like a trained poodle. After Lord Beaconsfield procured for his royal mistress the title of Empress of India, she became very fond of riding all round the back yard of Buckingham Palace in a *howdah* mounted on Jumbo's back, the Prime Minister sitting at the same time on the elephant's neck and acting as *mahout*. Of course, the matter was carefully kept from the knowledge of Liberal statesmen, and, indeed, would probably never have been known outside of the palace had not Jumbo managed to entangle his trunk with a clothes-line one Monday morning, the result of which was that he became frightened, raced around the yard, upsetting a chicken-coop and a laundress with a basket of clothes, and finally throwing both the Empress and the *mahout*, and necessitating the assistance of three policemen to secure him and conduct him to his kennel.

> Everybody who has been much in London during the last thirty years can testify to the truth of Mr Barnum's assertion that Jumbo has been ridden by the royal family. There was a time when the sagacious beast walked through St. James's Park every afternoon with the royal Princes and Princesses on his back. After a while their number increased to such an extent that Lord Palmerston was about to bring a bill before the House of Commons for an appropriation to pay the cost of building an extension to Jumbo's back large enough—in Sir William Paxton's estimation—to hold all existing and probable Princes and Princesses up to and including the year 1875, but the elephant having suddenly shown signs of a desire to throw most of the royal family into the lake, he was presented to the Zoological Society, and Lord Palmerston did not bring in the contemplated bill.

Continuing with tongue in cheek, the *New York Times* chided Barnum for callous disregard of British feelings, royal and common, and asked 'what has been able to work this complete and terrible change in the moral character of the once reasonable, upright, and kindly Barnum'.

Barnum replied instantly from the Madison Square Garden and his letter to the Editor was published next day under the heading 'The Repentant Barnum':

> Had I known positively that all the interesting facts detailed in your editorial on Jumbo in this morning's *Times* regarding his loving intimacy with Queen Victoria were indubitably true, (and they can no longer be doubted) I might have relented at the last moment and left the great pet of the palace in her Majesty's dominions. We all know that the Queen's attachment to Jumbo was so ardent that for years there could be no sleep on the royal couch until Jumbo had sounded his trumpet 'good night' from the Windsor Park or the back yard of Buckingham Palace, but I confess to some doubts concerning the Queen's riding on Jumbo's

RECEPTION IN NEW YORK.
Hurrah! hurrah! the sailors cried, when they Columbia's shores espied,
And all prepared for heavy work and gave me landing at New York.
When all the people came to view the monster from the London Zoo

IN AMERICAN COSTUME.
And when the Yankees saw my size, they opened their astonished eyes.
The gents with pride puffed at their pipes and dressed me up with stars and stripes
While joy-bells rang and ladies smiled and every child with joy was wild

back while Lord Beaconsfield, as a devoted Prime Minister, guided the monster by sitting astride his neck. This fact now being verified by your editorial, I shall shorten Jumbo's stay in America a month if possible and start back to England with him in October instead of November next, in order to assuage the

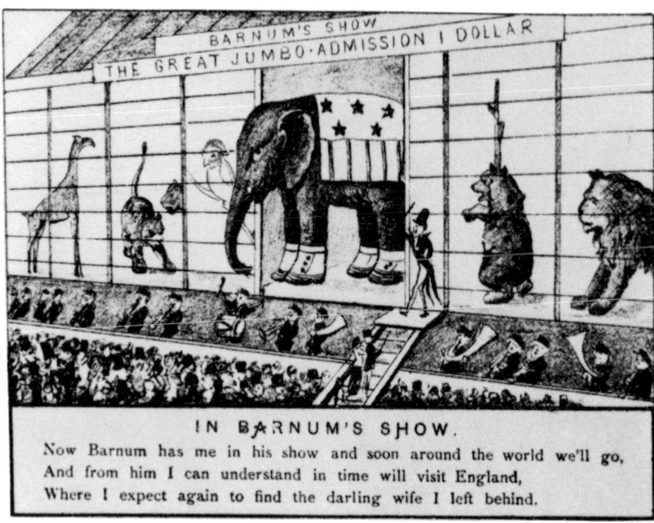

IN BARNUM'S SHOW.
Now Barnum has me in his show and soon around the world we'll go,
And from him I can understand in time will visit England,
Where I expect again to find the darling wife I left behind.

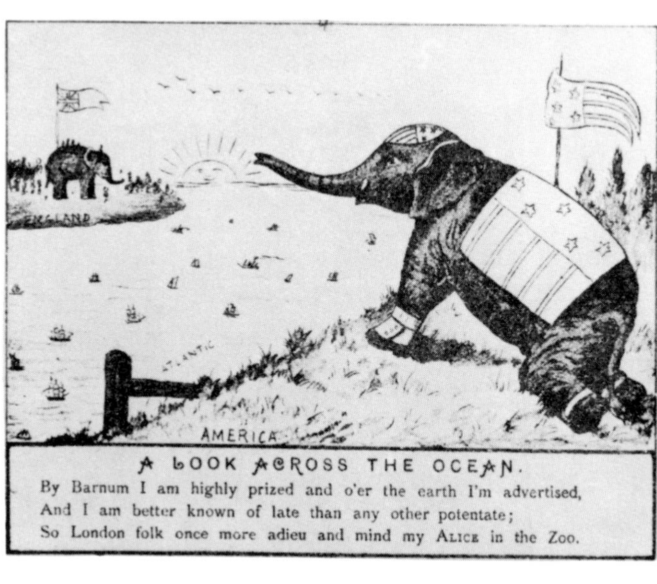

A LOOK ACROSS THE OCEAN.
By Barnum I am highly prized and o'er the earth I'm advertised,
And I am better known of late than any other potentate;
So London folk once more adieu and mind my ALICE in the Zoo.

royal grief and stop the flow of royal tears. I hope by this step to redeem my 'moral character', and not entirely to lose a reputation for at least ordinary benevolence and a kind 'fellow-feeling'. Meanwhile, from the most disinterested motives, and purely for the public good, I will whisper that Jumbo 'the largest and noblest animal on the face of the earth', is being exhibited at this Garden to 20,000 delighted citizens daily—'for ten days longer'. P. T. Barnum

Jumbo had spent his first night on American soil resting in his crate outside the Garden. As early morning New York stirred into life, and the newspapers announcing his arrival appeared on the streets, he was about to leave forever the crate which had been the focus of so much attention when it stood in the enclosure outside his old home in Regent's Park. Over the last few weeks he had experienced something of the Barnum style, and on the previous night he had even had a sniff of Broadway. Now when he walked out of the crate and through the entrance to the Garden he would break the last link with the long years of quiet routine in the London Zoo, and he and his old friend Scott would be starting a wandering life in the razzle-dazzle of the Greatest Show on Earth.

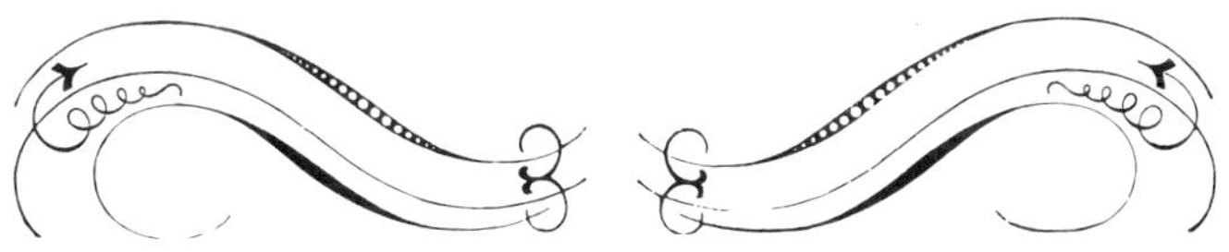

The Greatest Show on Earth

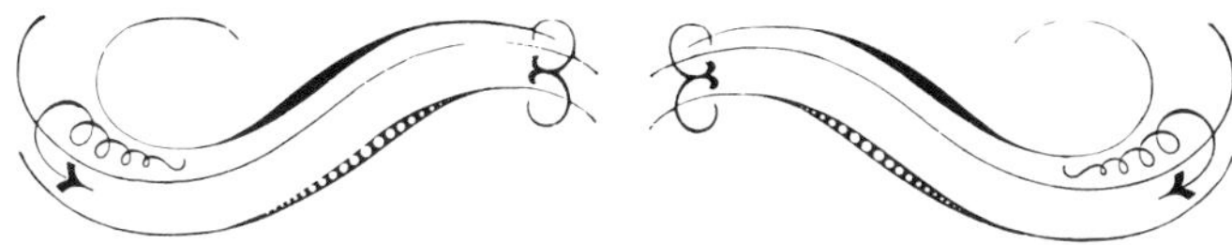

At daybreak on the morning after Jumbo disembarked, a crowd of circus hands issued out of the Fourth Avenue entrance of the Madison Square Garden and, under the direction of Bailey and Hutchinson, set about getting the elephant inside the building which housed the circus during its regular season in New York. The great arena had recently undergone considerable reconstruction. Partitions had been removed to make huge rooms for the museum and menagerie, the stabling under the tiers of seats had been enlarged to accommodate extra animals, and the forty-foot-wide track running round the arena had been extended.

Barnum himself was not present. He played little or no part in the day-to-day organisation of the circus, although many of the public still called it 'Barnum's'. The show was run by Bailey and Hutchinson, and the old man's contribution was to spot sensational exhibits. But he resented —sometimes to the point of litigation—suggestions that he did little more than sell his name and reputation to the circus.

The doors to the Garden were open wide and the fanlight removed, but the crate still proved too big to pass through. It was left in the entrance and the bars knocked out at the front so that Jumbo could see clearly into the backstage area and, if he so minded, walk out of his box and into his new home.

Once the box was open the little group of circus people watched it expectantly. There was a long pause, and then Jumbo put a tentative foot onto the ground. He quickly drew it back into the box, and shortly afterwards did the same with his other foot, testing the earth that he had not touched for weeks. It had been decided that he should be given every chance to take kindly to his new surroundings, and not be rushed in any way. He was neither tempted with fruit nor goaded with the elephant hook by the trainer of the Barnum herd. There was another long pause, with subdued chatter among the watchers, and then slowly Jumbo walked a few paces out of the crate and stopped and stretched. Scott at once moved to his head, spoke to him, and kept him standing there a few minutes.

The famous elephant was for the first time fully revealed on American soil, no longer just a big box with a shadowy occupant and a disembodied trunk, but a living creature with shape and texture, standing free and uncluttered, and gazing back at the circus people as they ran their knowledgeable eyes up and over the huge bulk. In the past they had seen the arrival of many well-publicised new marvels, and on this occasion there was no sense of disappointment. What particularly impressed these sophisticated observers, who saw elephants every day, was Jumbo's tallness. He seemed to have grown bigger than the box which had contained him. Some thought he looked as though he were on stilts, and one of those present compared him with a popular negro entertainer of the time who was noted for his length of leg accentuated by the striped trousers of his minstrel costume.

When Scott decided that the elephant had been given long enough to find his feet he led him slowly forward into the dressing area beyond which lay the great arena. There was an immediate alarming setback when thin wooden flooring, laid directly on the ground, broke under the weight. Jumbo's feet did not penetrate the splintered planking, but he retreated at once. Fortunately, though, he was not too badly frightened, and he walked forward again as soon as a firm pathway of heavy timber had been laid for him.

When he came out onto the track at the perimeter of the

great arena he looked about him, took a few steps, and then caused further consternation by kneeling down and collapsing on his side to lie quite still. He was however doing no more than enjoying a position denied to him for the past month. He lay there for some minutes, occasionally wafting his trunk lazily through the air, and rolling one bright eye round at the banks of empty seats and the lights and trapezes high above. Then he decided that he had rested enough and got slowly to his feet and moved forward again. He was led around the track past the closed doors of the elephant stables, but he did not appear to sense the presence there of twenty or more of his Indian cousins. He was to be housed in separate quarters some distance from the main herd. Sharing this accommodation, but in an enclosure well removed from Jumbo's, was a female elephant and her baby which had very recently been born in the circus winter quarters at Bridgeport. They showed some signs of excitement when he came through the doors but settled down again when he was led to his own enclosure on the far side of the big room. The rails around this enclosure were of a strength intended to restrain the public on their side rather than the elephant on the other, so Jumbo was tethered by attaching the chain on his hind leg to a heavy stake driven deep into the ground.

Here, with Jumbo at last safely installed in the circus, the showmen were able to stand and contemplate their new star with wonder and satisfaction, and speculate upon the impact he would have upon the public at the afternoon matinée. The mood did not last long. Jumbo, on his side of the rail, contemplated the showmen for a while and then apparently decided that they were an interesting bunch who might possibly have buns or oranges about their persons. He took one friendly stride towards them and the tethering stake came out of the ground like the stalk of a ripe strawberry. Blacksmiths were summoned at the trot. They rapidly put together, and firmly fixed in the enclosure, a massive iron structure to which Jumbo's chain was now more securely attached.

As the time of the afternoon performance approached,

the bustle of preparation, and the sound of music outside, aroused Jumbo's pleasurable interest. When the public was admitted to the Garden there was a rush to see Jumbo, who, Scott reported, clearly enjoyed having a crowd around the rails of his enclosure. There were more big crowds at the evening performance— the day's attendance was the best since the show opened—and Jumbo again held court in a well-behaved and impressive manner. Barnum's colleagues began to feel optimistic that their new acquisition would bring more dollars than trouble. Very soon Jumbo was introduced into the circus proper, although his role during the show remained that of exhibit rather than performer.

Many of the titles of the individual acts proclaimed on the circus posters would not have stood close investigation, but the most extravagant claim of all—The Greatest Show on Earth—perhaps had most justification. There were three separate rings, and surrounding them the race track, forty feet wide and nearly four hundred yards long. Filling these four great show areas with a fast-moving spectacle of dazzling complexity were nearly four hundred performers, over three hundred horses, score upon score of other animals, and several brass bands to add a riot of sound to a kaleidoscope of colour under the brilliant electric lights.

All the rings were in use simultaneously, and sometimes on the track there would also be a chariot race, Ben Hur style, or perhaps a parade of zebras, giraffes, or deer, harnessed to golden carts and carriages. The curiosities on display were gathered from all over the world, and if some of them came from nearer home, their names suggested otherwise:[1] the Wild Men of Borneo; the African Marimba Band, said to have been found by H. M. Stanley; Constantine the Greek, who was tattooed on every conceivable part of his body—indeed on every part; the Siamese Twins; General Tom Thumb; the Two-Headed Negro Girl; the Chinese Giant. Some of the curiosities did little more than appear in one of the rings, others had worked up some sort of performance to display their peculiarity, and there were speciality acts like Mademoiselle Zazel who was shot out of a cannon and caught by a man hanging from a trapeze high in the air. There were those performers who relied upon skill rather than curiosity: jugglers, wire-walkers, clowns, and acrobats. The equestrian acts were almost a self-contained show: horses drilling, dancing, counting, and answering questions, and daring riders performing all manner of tricks on, under, and beside their mounts. Some of the more ferocious animals were displayed in cages, while others did tricks under the control, and sometimes, thrillingly, almost appearing to be out of the control, of their intrepid trainers. With so many things to see at once, people in the audience were quite bewildered as they sat through a dream-like fantasia of unconnected sensations: amusing, amazing, frightening and grotesque.

When Jumbo was introduced into the show he was given the most prominent place in the parade of the elephants. The recent amalgamation of Barnum's circus with that of Bailey and Hutchinson, in March 1881, had brought together a collection of nearly thirty elephants, and when they lumbered ponderously into the ring in a

Courier Co.
BUFFALO. N.Y. U.S.A.
THE ENORMOUS HORSE FAIR
SHOWING THE VAST CAVALCADE OF HIGH-CLASS STOCK OWNED & EXHIBITED BY THE GREAT BARNUM & BAILEY SHOW
AN ACTUAL SCENE ON THE GREAT HIPPODROME TRACK. OVER 400 CHOICE THOROUGHBREDS FROM ALL PARTS OF THE WORLD

Three-ring circus in New York

disciplined line, with the enormous figure of Jumbo at the head, the crowd was thrilled by such an accumulation of wild power which amply satisfied any primeval need for the reassuring sight of monsters subdued. At the tail of the parade, when the audience's first fear had given way to interest and amusement, came two baby elephants to excite their sentimental affection.

The first of these two calves had been born before the amalgamation of the two circuses, and Barnum had been exceptionally jealous that his rivals had beaten him in producing so great an attraction. He had offered to buy mother and calf from Bailey and Hutchinson but they refused and published his offer in advertisements as an indication to the public of the superiority of their show. The baby elephant had been a significant item in bringing about the merger of the two circuses, and Barnum was delighted when a second calf was born soon afterwards. He felt that it helped justify his claim to be an expert in the management of elephants, and one who would succeed with Jumbo where the London Zoo had failed, or, more correctly, feared they would fail.

When he had led the elephants into and around the ring, Jumbo stood on one side watching, with obvious attention and interest, as the others went through their performance. A roll was called and each elephant acknowledged his name, then some stood on their forelegs, others played on a see-saw, some balanced on barrels, and Tom Thumb, the small clown elephant, did his drunken turn with waiter and keeper. Before and after the show Jumbo would be the centre of attention when, with a wooden bench on his back and Scott at his head, he would give rides to children just as he had done in Regent's Park, and with just as much success.

Barnum visited England in 1883 and stayed in Southport, near the family home of his second wife, whom he had married nine years before when he was sixty-four and she twenty-four. He was prevailed upon to address a gathering in the Winter Gardens there, to give a first-hand account of how Jumbo was settling to his new life in America.

Barnum gave his own description of the day Jumbo first entered Madison Square Garden:

> Jumbo, to the delight of the people across the water, arrived in perfect health, and amidst much rejoicing. The day following he was introduced to my herd of elephants, numbering, without him twenty-two, and I can assure you the meeting, the like of which was never seen before, and, possibly, will never be witnessed again, was a most interesting one for all who took part in it. Jumbo was delighted, and his future companions expressed their gratification by unmistakable signs of pleasure. The herd was drawn up in column, and Mr Jumbo was marched along the line, saluting each one he came to. They seized each others' trunks, embraced, and altogether showed, as I have said, great delight at making a new acquaintance. He was soon at home, and was not long before he selected his favourite of the other sex, and already he has shown a particular liking for three or four out of the females, and I have no doubt that before long he will be 'setting his cap' at the others.

Jumbo, Tom Thumb, and others

This is a rather more colourful account than is reported elsewhere but, as Barnum himself said, 'I am nothing but a showman, ladies and gentlemen, and never pretend to be anything else. Let me conclude by saying that, through me, Jumbo presents his compliments to the whole British nation, and I, in return, shall take yours back to him.'[2]

Barnum was particularly pleased to be able to tell his British audience that Jumbo's presence had been responsible for a general increase of about five hundred pounds per day in the circus takings, and that in the first three days at the Garden he had brought in enough to cover the cost of his purchase. Barnum attributed much of this success to publicity. His own, of course, was on a scale appropriate to its subject, but he was much helped by the pamphleteers and souvenir merchants. They rushed out their tawdry goods to turn a quick profit for themselves from another man's sensation, and in so doing fed the fever. In London, one paper[3] had complained of 'Jumbos in india-rubber, Jumbos in terra cotta, Jumbos in porcelain, Jumbos in ivory, Jumbos in meerschaum. Whoever has a figure of an elephant of any sort or size among his stock now sticks it in his shop window and labels it Jumbo.' There had been insufficient time to design and make anything of substance, so these early souvenirs were generally either old stock or rubbish. When Jumbo had been some months in the United States it was possible, on both sides of the Atlantic, to gratify a wish for souvenirs of greater merit.

Arthur Sketchley, the humorous writer, quickly produced another volume in his 'Mrs Brown' series,[4] *Mrs Brown on Jumbo* published 'in fancy boards at One Shilling'. Mrs Brown, a far-sighted and long-winded cockney chauvinist, amused the British public with comment on current affairs expressed in sentences, of which this is one of the shorter examples:

> No doubt Queen Wictorier would 'ave telegraffed to Jumbo, to say as she were sorry as he'd been put out of

the way about goin' to Merryker, and as she wouldn't allow 'im to be tampered with by a lot of Yankee Doodle rebels as is wot 'er grandfather, Old King George, always would call 'em, to 'is dyin' day, as some says, he drove 'em into, by bein' that obstinate about their tea, as were foolishness, no doubt, but it's all for the best, as the sayin' is, cos they'd 'ave give us a good deal of trouble; the same as them Colonials, as 'ad better be cut adrift, as'll be sure to throw us over, when we've served their turn, as is 'uman natur all over the world.

The porcelain, glass, and other Jumbo statuary produced at this time is perhaps more to modern taste than Mrs Brown, at any rate sufficiently so to attract the

Staffordshire Souvenir of Jumbo

attention of collectors today. There is, in the Natural History Division of the British Museum at South Kensington, an excellent two-foot-high Jumbo by W. Prehn which has been adopted as the type model for *Elephas Africanus Rothschildi*.[5] In less scientific style, the Staffordshire Pottery produced commemorative pieces, one standing about twenty-eight centimetres high, and a smaller one sitting down, each of them bearing the name Jumbo.[6] In America, the Jumbo craze fell within the period when interesting patterns of early pressed glass tableware were being produced.[7] One sought-after piece was a butter dish with a frosted glass elephant labelled Jumbo as the knob on the lid. Another was a spoonholder of patented design meant to stand on the table, and consisting of an ornate glass column over a foot high surmounted by a frosted Jumbo and supporting a decorated circular glass canopy from which hung a dozen spoons. Ephemera of little value were still produced long after Jumbo arrived in America, but not on the scale of the original international craze: cards like cigarette cards given away with sewing thread, charms, photographs, and paper hats. Often such material was the result of local enterprise associated with the arrival of the Barnum circus in town, or sometimes it was sold to children at the circus itself.

The circus season in Madison Square Garden lasted thirty days and then the show went on tour, travelling throughout the eastern United States and parts of Canada by rail. It was a very tough schedule. They usually gave two shows a day, staying two days each in Boston, Chicago and Philadelphia; six days in Cincinnati and St Louis; two days in Washington, Baltimore, and four or five other towns; but most often they stayed just one day and then travelled on overnight, fifty or a hundred miles to the next town which had more than thirty thousand inhabitants.

The circus had its own rolling stock: nearly a hundred carriages and freight cars that were usually made up into three or four separate trains. Barnum warned the public that they should come to see Jumbo before he grew too big for the railway tunnels. During the tour there might be over a hundred night rail journeys. On these occasions the animals—some walking, some in cages—would be taken back to the railway siding immediately after their evening performance and loaded onto the train. Then the tents would be struck, equipment dismantled, and all packed into circus wagons and put onto flat-top railway trucks as quickly as possible so that everything could arrive at the next town in time to go through the whole smooth routine in reverse at first light the following day. The principal organiser of this gigantic packing and transport operation was Bailey, of whom it was said[8] that the German High Command sent its Quartermaster General to travel with his circus and learn something about the rapid transport and deployment by rail of large quantities of men, animals, and equipment.

When they arrived at a new stand, Jumbo and all the other elephants would walk in the early morning from the railway to the showground, often a distance of a mile or two, and back again at about ten o'clock at night. The show horses, and even camels and elephants, were used to lift loads and pull wagons just as the human performers did their share of the drudgery, with the trapeze and high-wire men scrambling nimbly about high up in the roof of the tent, fixing poles, canvas, and wires. But Barnum declared that, as patriarch of the herd, Jumbo was never called upon to do any haulage work. This was an indulgence prompted as much by expediency as by seniority, since African elephants take slowly to labouring duties, and Jumbo had never been trained to such work.

Jumbo travelled in a railway van made specially for him by the Pennsylvania Railroad Company. The vehicle was mounted on two six-wheeled bogies and it was carefully constructed to have just sufficient clearance at bridges, tunnels, and sharp curves. Jumbo's Palace Car, as it was called, was richly painted in gold and red, with double entrance doors in the middle, reaching almost down to the track. Scott's quarters were in the same van, and when on tour he and Jumbo lived, ate, and slept there. Last thing at night before getting into his bunk, Scott used to treat himself to a bottle of beer. He would drink rather more than half and then give the remainder to Jumbo. One night, according to an oft-told story, Scott drank his half and then went to bed, forgetting for some reason to give his companion the remainder. Jumbo waited for what he clearly thought was a reasonable time, but still Scott lay in his bunk. Eventually the elephant reached out and gently lifted his keeper out of bed and put him down on the floor. Scott took the hint, Jumbo got his belated night-cap, and both passed the rest of the night as peacefully as is possible on a moving train.

One night when they were on the move between towns Scott was preparing for bed in the big van when another train passed at high speed in the opposite direction. As it did so its engine gave a shrill whistle which so startled Jumbo that he stumbled against Scott and badly bruised him. The elephant had no idea what he had done, and during the three or four days that Scott was away re-cuperating he fretted and pined for his old keeper.

THE PRIDE AND GLORY OF ENGLAND, AND GUEST OF AMERICA.

Barnum publicity

Week after week of the unremitting routine of pack, travel and perform had its effect upon the whole circus. Men and women looked forward to the months of relaxation at Bridgeport, Connecticut, and when they got there the animals appreciated the peace and comfort of the large specially heated buildings which housed them at Barnum's enormous permanent winter site. For the first few weeks there most were preoccupied with the enjoyment of rest, good food eaten in leisurely style, and nights free from the shake and rattle of the railway.

The soft living at Bridgeport soon brought the animals back into first-class condition; it put a bloom on their coats and a gleam in their eyes that had the circus proprietors consulting the calendar and considering the potential value of a baby of the species before deciding who should consort with whom. Columbia, the first elephant born in captivity in America or Europe, had been the pride of Bailey and Hutchinson before the amalgamation with Barnum, and she was followed a couple of years later by the first baby elephant born in the joint circus, and named, appropriately, Bridgeport.

But life in winter quarters was not all rest and self-indulgence. There was a permanent training ring where the animals were kept up to the mark in their old tricks and taught new ones for the coming season. A visitor described such a training session for the elephants: 'Here is a big fellow who is taught to go through the motion of sanding his feet on a small platform before mounting the cask he is to roll around the ring . . . . As several of his brethren are simultaneously busy in the ring, one ringing a handbell with tumultuous zeal, another turning a hand-organ for all he is worth, and others making pyramids and statues of "theirselves", this fellow, finding the pretence of sanding his feet a cheap substitute for his cask practice, solemnly continues it until a sharp jab of a metal point calls him to his duty.' Some of the animals were required to do labouring work from time to time during the winter, shifting caravans and pulling carts. For really demanding tasks the elephants were sometimes brought out, and on one such occasion a couple of them caught a chill from working in the cold. That evening they began to shake and shiver, and each animal was given three large bottles of whisky as a homely remedy. The next morning when the keepers went in, all the elephants put on an attack of the shivers and only reverted to a normal healthy stance when it became quite clear that this was not a performance which automatically attracted a round of drinks.

Jumbo was not required to do any work in or out of the training ring, and although he thrived on the rest and good food it is possible that he became a little bored with his own society. He was confined in a stable for long periods much as he had been at the London Zoo, and, just as he had done there, he attacked the reinforced wooden wall of his compartment one night and knocked a hole in it. Apart from this he showed no sign under American management of the outbursts which had so alarmed the authorities in England.

Barnum claimed that Jumbo was still growing, which was true, and that in less than eighteen months after coming from England he had shot up five inches in height and put on a ton in weight. This was almost certainly not true. His broken tusks had undoubtedly grown several inches, and it was thought that this was because he no longer wore them away scraping at a brick wall as he had done in London.

There had always been considerable speculation among the general public about Jumbo's height and weight, and the impressive dimensions of various parts of his body. When he left London he was almost certainly nearly eleven feet tall and weighed six tons. But after his arrival in the United States, Barnum always made much of his size and the rate at which he was growing, while at the same time frustrating any serious attempt to establish his true height.

One of the most persistent enquirers after truth in this matter, and one well qualified to establish it, was Dr Hornaday, a distinguished American zoologist. In Washington in 1883 Hornaday managed to get a card from

Barnum giving him permission to measure Jumbo: the card was endorsed 'provided Mr Bailey consents'. Barnum and Hornaday parted, each happy about the outcome of the interview, although Barnum had more reason for confidence. Hornaday recorded[9] that when the card was presented to Bailey 'his indignation was as colossal as the great pachyderm. "*Measure* Jumbo? *In*deed!"'

Dr Hornaday was not the only thwarted measurer at this time. Members of the circus wanted to know the secret of Jumbo's height, but the ban was applied to them with equal rigour. Two performers, more enterprising than the rest, devised a novel form of mensuration to be carried out during a performance, in full view of circus officials and the public, without anyone realising what was happening. Details of the remarkable measurement were passed on to Dr Hornaday, some twenty-eight years later.

One of the two conspirators, named Elder, was a pole-vaulter—a type of athlete rare enough in 1883 to be a circus curiosity—and the scheme depended upon the cunning use of his pole. Elder performed his prodigous leaps in the same ring at Madison Square Garden where

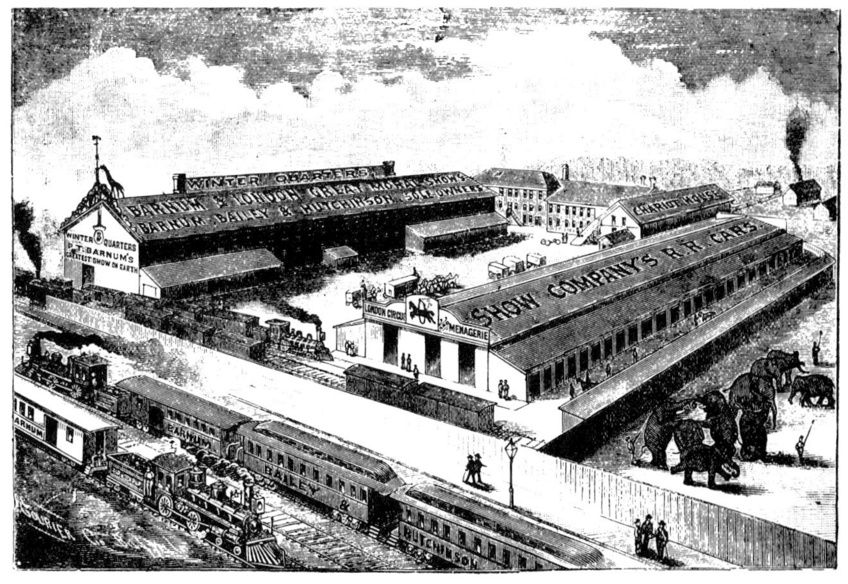

Winter quarters of the Great London-Barnum Show

Jumbo stood in massive inactivity watching the frenzy of entertainment going on all around. The plan was that Elder, during his warming-up exercises, should land close by the side of Jumbo and stand casually there with his pole held carefully in a vertical position. The other conspirator would meanwhile take up a position nearby, ready, like the other half of a surveying pair, to note the point on the pole that coincided with Jumbo's highest point, and to remember it, so that the length of the pole to that point could later be measured. The result of this single determination of height, distinguished more for daring than precision, was ten foot nine inches. This rather modest figure probably did not give Jumbo, and Barnum, benefit of parallax. A piece of simple and plausible trigonometry suggests that several inches should be added, and that Jumbo was probably a shade over eleven feet tall.

But at this time, at the end of 1883, Barnum had another secret about Jumbo to be guarded even more closely. He believed that the elephant was far from well, and his letters reveal that he was making plans to cope with the possibility of Jumbo's sudden death. One American newspaper, over seventy years later, in 1954,[10] 'revealed', under a sensational headline that might have been written by the old showman himself, that Barnum had arranged for Jumbo to be secretly shot.

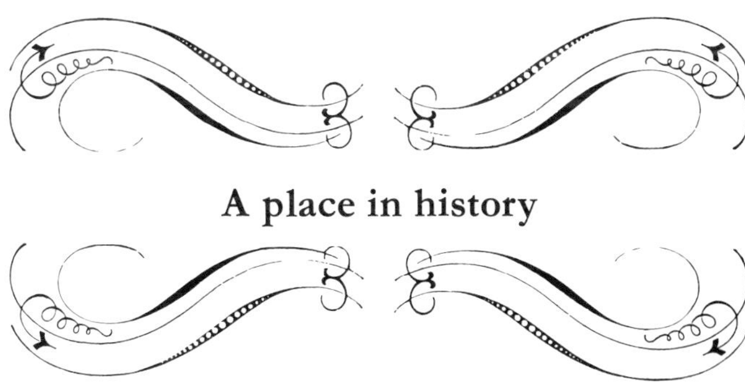

A place in history

During 1883, after a year or so of circus life, it was evident to Scott and Newman and other of Barnum's employees, that Jumbo was ailing. He showed physical symptoms similar to those which Bartlett had noticed years before in London when the elephant's system had been poisoned by the abscesses at the roots of his broken tusks. He was listless, off his feed, suffered digestive disturbance, and was reluctant to lie down. On this occasion however there was no such obvious cause for the illness and no possibility of quick remedial surgery. None of the simple medical remedies that were tried seemed to have any effect upon Jumbo's chronic debility.

If he had been suffering from some serious internal disease it is unlikely that the veterinary knowledge then available would have been adequate to diagnose it. In the absence of any positive evidence of this kind the most likely reason for Jumbo's decline was probably dietary—not so much a deficiency in the food provided by the circus as the possibility that something, or an accumulation of things, given to him by a cruelly ignorant public was damaging his stomach or otherwise poisoning him.

Jumbo's illness was kept secret from the public and he still appeared regularly at circus performances. But Barnum, who had so strongly and successfully promoted the great elephant as the outstanding attraction of his show, was much concerned about the effect his death might have upon attendances. Without Jumbo his show would be like the Tower of London without the Crown Jewels or Madame Tussaud's without the Chamber of Horrors. Barnum felt that the Greatest Show on Earth was now so closely associated with Jumbo that if he died it would be essential to try to achieve at least some illusion of the continuity of his presence. He believed that he knew the taste and sentiment of the public at the time and he planned accordingly. What he had in mind was that Jumbo, stuffed, and Jumbo's 'widow' should sustain the legend if Jumbo died. He wrote to Ward,[1] an American expert on the preservation of animal bodies, saying that he had given instructions that if the elephant died '(which Heaven forbid) you must be telegraphed immediately, and I hope you will lose no time in saving his skin and skeleton'. At about the same time he made contact with Bartlett about another purchase from the London Zoo where Jumbo had been replaced by a young African elephant, called Jingo. The Superintendent addressed a memo[2] to Sclater, the Secretary of the Zoological Society: 'Will you authorize me to sell Alice the female African Elephant and at what price? I have seen Mr Barnum and I think I can manage to dispose of the Elephant but I must let him know immediately the terms.'

Barnum recognised that Alice and the mounted skin of Jumbo might arouse some public interest, but they would be no more than the relics of an old box office sensation, like some passé stage star—worth a place on the bill, but only in the smaller print. A top of the bill attraction in the Jumbo mould would be needed if the great elephant did die, so Barnum, like many a famous old man, tried to repeat the trick which had brought him fame. In 1883 he managed, 'with the permission of the King of Siam', to buy Toung Taloung, a 'sacred' white elephant which was shipped to London, where it was accommodated temporarily in Jumbo's old house at the Zoo.

Travellers' tales of mysterious oriental religions fascinated nineteenth-century Britons and Americans, and they had taken the phrase 'white elephant' into the language to describe a useless object, although for the citizen of Siam it had the more sinister meaning of a crippling financial incubus. So extravagantly lavish was the treatment which tradition demanded for the white elephant that only the king could afford it, and if a Siamese noble incurred royal disfavour then he might be given one of the sacred beasts and thus deliberately ruined. Mrs Leonowens—Anna, the English governess of the King of Siam's children—wrote of the white elephant in 1870:[3]

A place in history

> When the governor of a province of Siam is notified of the appearance of a white elephant within his bailiwick, he immediately commands that prayers and offerings shall be made in all the temples, while he sends out a formidable expedition of hunters and slaves to take the precious beast, and bring it in in triumph. As soon as he is informed of its capture, a special messenger is despatched to inform the King of its sex, probable age, size, complexion, deportment, looks, and ways; and in the presence of his Majesty this bearer of glorious tidings undergoes the painfully pleasant operation of having his mouth, ears, and nostrils stuffed with gold . . . . [the elephant] is conducted with great pomp to his sumptuous quarters within the precincts of the first king's palace, where he is received by his own court of officers, attendants and slaves, who install him in his fine lodgings, and at once proceed to robe and decorate him. First, the court jeweller rings his tremendous tusks with massive gold, crowns him with a diadem of beaten gold of perfect purity, and adorns his burly neck with heavy golden chains.

To the unprejudiced observer the most remarkable thing about the white elephant was the fact that it was grey with pink spots—the pink patches were on the head, ears, trunk, and chest, but the toenails were white. When Toung Taloung arrived in London *The Spectator*[4] commented,

> Mr Barnum, misled by the enthusiasm manifested in this country for Jumbo, evidently thinks that the

> English are susceptible about elephants, and has sent over a beast purchased in Burmah, which he declares to be one of the 'white' variety held there to be semi-sacred. The daily journals are helping him, and publishing minute accounts of the creature, and of the 'gentle' way in which it walks up gangways, but we suspect he will be disappointed. The public fancies that a white elephant is white, and will hold that a slate-coloured brute with pink patches, not eight feet high, and not otherwise remarkable, is not the animal it is looking for. Jumbo was really the biggest beast existing in the world, for people never think of a whale as a beast, though it is one, and the common folk admired him as such; but Toung is neither big nor beautiful, nor anything else, except possibly 'sacred' among a people who are less known in England than any race in Asia. Mr Barnum should give some sharp Yankee chemist a few thousand dollars to invent a new bleaching process, and then show his elephant in the colours which the populace expect.

The RSPCA, too, felt that Barnum was trying too soon to take London for a second ride over familar country. The Society's magazine *Animal World* remarked,[5] 'The glamour and mystery business is never forgotten by Mr Barnum; and, consequently, besides this preliminary puffing, we are told that two Buddhist priests are *en route*, and, with certain interesting religious forms, will be shown to the public, also, at the Gardens.'

This pseudo-religious side-show to be put on at the Zoo suggested that Barnum's agents were worried that their elephant was not, on his own, sufficient attraction. They were in truth disappointed with his colour, and, lacking a 'Sharp Yankee chemist', they subjected him to a prolonged bathing and scrubbing which did no more than give him a a chill so that he had to be given a bottle of brandy, for which he showed a liking deemed unbecoming in a supposed Buddhist dignitary. Barnum's men were correct in fearing that the stunt was falling flat. *Animal World*[6] reported public reaction:

> Barnum's 'sacred white' elephant, who is neither sacred nor white, is still on view at the Zoological Gardens, Regent's Park. He stands all day long in Jumbo's

BOSTON, ON COLOSSEUM GROUNDS, FOR A BRIEF SEASON, COMMENCING MONDAY, JUNE 16
History of the
$ 200.000.
SACRED WHITE ELEPHANT.
ETHNOLOGICAL·CONGRESS·OF·
SAVAGE AND BARBAROUS
TRIBES
·AND·BOOK·OF·
JUMBO.
The Courier Company Show Printing House, Buffalo, N. Y. The Largest in the World; Fire-Proof.

Programme of attraction.

stall, with green cloth drapery around him to give effect to his colour, to do honour to his high rank, or to keep up the glamour of a nineteenth-century elephantine bubble. As often as we have been there, the same remark has rolled off the tongue of visitors on their approaching him—'What a shame to call him white! It is a swindle!'

There were suggestions that the Press, the Zoo, and Barnum had conspired to try to raise a public ferment. Fellows of the Zoological Society of London complained to the Council, particularly about the costumed Burmese religious attendants. Many called for a prompt severance of the links with Barnum, saying for instance that the Society had been 'held responsible for every mendacious statement concerning Mr Barnum's elephant by his agent'. One angry member even declared that Barnum's employee had the previous night, 'grossly insulted me and threatened to smash my face with his "diamond" ring'. The protests had some effect upon the Council of the Zoological Society: Barnum's agents were told that no ceremonials were to take place with the Burmese, and the negotiations about the despatch of Alice to America appear to have been suspended when almost complete.

There were no great scenes when the white elephant left London for America aboard the *Lydian Monarch*. When the vessel arrived in New York, Barnum went out in a tug with a party of guests to board her at the Quarantine station. They viewed the beast and, at a formal luncheon for his guests and the Press, Barnum did his best to take the minds of the reporters off the inescapable sense of anti-climax by recounting details of thrilling plots and counter-plots involved in securing the animal and whisking it away from its homeland.

The public never showed great interest in Toung Taloung when he joined Jumbo in the show, in spite of a flood of typical Barnum advertising. It was ironic that an arch-rival of Barnum, who had out-witted him in several important circus deals, should be more successful when he exhibited a white elephant of his own.[7] The great advantage of the rival elephant was that it was clearly and totally white, but not genuinely so. At a Press reception to display this animal a journalist managed to rub its flank with a wet sponge and confirm his suspicion that it was painted. The reporter did not publish his discovery, but told Barnum, who made sure that the public was kept well informed of the nature of the fake. Nevertheless people preferred to see a fake white elephant that was white rather than a genuine one that was grey with pink spots.

Sharing the top of the bill, on tour with Jumbo and the Sacred White Elephant in 1884 and 1885, was what was described on the posters as 'The Ethnological Congress of Savage and Barbarous Tribes. 100 Rude and Savage Representatives, Fanatical and Pagan Idolators, Bestial and Fierce Human Beings. Every rude barbarian presented exactly as described in history—no curtailment in habits or customs and no exaggeration. Appeals directly to the intelligence of the public and the educated of all classes.' Among the exhibits gathered—'only after three years of danger and labor, and two fortunes expended'—were Dancing Nautch Girls, Australian Cannibals, Cetewayo's Zulu Braves, American Red Men of the tribes who opposed Gallant Custer in his Last Fight, and Meek and Gentle People of the Laos Country.

In 1882 when London was seething about the deal between Barnum and the Zoo, the United States Ambassador to the Court of St James had remarked that the only cause of contention between the British and American people appeared to be the sale of Jumbo. But as the wound left by his removal from England healed, and his genial presence engaged the affection of the townspeople of America, Jumbo became one of those living links which bind together the two countries quite independently of the best and worst efforts of politicians and diplomats.

British 'exiles' in the United States were as delighted to see Jumbo as they were to hear an English accent in the street. A distinguished looking English gentleman visiting the Madison Square Garden said that he had come to see the elephant on which he had ridden as a boy in Regent's Park. At Oswego, on the American shore of Lake Ontario, a large group of visitors to the circus was standing in front of Jumbo's enclosure feeding him titbits. Towards the back of the crowd was an elderly woman who was trying to get near enough to give him something. Jumbo was graciously selecting what attracted him most from the offerings held out by many eager hands close-by. Suddenly he stopped feeding for a moment, then moved as far as his chain would allow to the front of the enclosure, and stretched out his trunk towards the elderly woman, accepting her food and no other. She was allowed by the crowd to come forward and Scott asked her if Jumbo had ever seen her before. '"Oh yes," replied the lady, "many is the time I have stood for an hour or more, and fed him with candy and nuts in the Zoo at London; but do you suppose he really remembers me?" "Of course he does," said the keeper. "Don't you see he will not notice anybody else? I knew the minute I saw him stop eating and look at the crowd that he knew someone."'

In 1884 a group of Jumbo's fans in the United States decided as an act of respect and goodwill to send a message to the Baroness Burdett-Coutts who had concerned herself with the elephant's welfare when he sailed from England. A satin banner was delivered to the Baroness in London printed with a poem, signed Jumbo, part of which read:

> The Americans—warm-hearted people—try
> With England's kindness to your slave to vie;
> But ah, those 'Gardens'! can I e'er forget,
> Where wondering thousands daily round me met?
> Still less that crowded steamer's deck, where you
> Honoured poor Jumbo with a last adieu?
> The weeping emigrants could kiss your hand,
> But I could only wave my trunk—and stand.

Towards the end of the 1885 touring season the circus was playing small towns in Canada, and the performers were beginning to look forward to the quiet days and restful nights of winter quarters back in Bridgeport. On the morning of Tuesday, 15 September 1885 they arrived at St Thomas, a little railway town in western Ontario with a population of about nine thousand. It was to be a day of much sadness.

A place in history

The site was not far from the railway yard, and the brightly painted circus vans were soon unloaded from their flat-top trucks and hauled out to the show-ground. The tents were pitched, and everywhere was a bustle of preparation for the first of the two shows. During the matinée a bare-back rider called Nicholls fell while attempting a trick he had done a hundred times before. Colleagues were swift to cover for him, and with so much going on in the three rings it was easy to divert the audience's attention from what looked to be no more than a trifling mishap. But the daring acrobat of moments before was badly injured and was dying as they carried his limp, spangled body out of the ring.

The show, of course, went on. Act followed act, as always, in a whirl of movement and noise, and the shouts and laughter of the audience came through the canvas walls of the big top to the quieter tents outside where the dead man was mourned. In the evening the audience for the second performance jumbled merrily into their seats, and the circus people smoothly carried out their public routine while holding at a distance their private knowledge. Hardly anything was changed by the man's death. As each act finished in the ring it made its way back to the railway yard to be loaded onto the train, ready for the ride through the night to another town and another show.

At about half-past nine in the evening the elephants reached the railway. The circus hands had removed a section of the fence so that it was possible to get their equipment and animals straight into the goods yard without going some distance up the road to a level crossing. Once inside the yard, the elephants were led along the railway track, by the side of the circus train which was standing on a parallel line. As they walked along, the circus train was immediately on their right, and on their left was a steeply sloping embankment dropping down almost eight feet to a field below. Twenty-nine of the elephants had been led along the track and loaded into their box-cars, and Scott was taking the last two, Jumbo and his little friend Tom Thumb, along the same way accompanied by a railwayman. Suddenly there was the sound of a train in the distance and then, about five hundred yards behind them, they saw the headlamp of a locomotive approaching down the hill. The horrified railwayman realised that it was on the track on which they were walking. Warning Scott, he ran back towards the on-coming train waving his flag.

Scott tried to make the two elephants turn left down the embankment, but they were frightened of the slope. So he quickly urged them forward into a trot, trying to reach the end of the circus train where they would be able to turn right and escape from the trap. The train bearing down on them—Special Freight No. 151, hauled by a Grand Trunk Railway locomotive—had been overlooked because it was not in the regular time-table. It was still several hundred yards away when the driver saw the running figure of the railwayman ahead of him, and the two elephants beyond. He threw the engine into reverse and blew three short blasts to call for brakes. This was a year or two before American freight trains were fitted with a modern braking system, and it was necessary for brakemen to turn by hand the big wheels on the individual box-cars which applied the brakes. There was not enough time to bring the train to rest. It screeched down the gradient in a shower of sparks and hit the running elephants when they were still half-a-dozen truck lengths from the end of the circus train and safety.

The little clown elephant, who was behind, was struck first and flung aside down the embankment. Then the locomotive shuddered as it hit Jumbo and came to a stop, tipped on one side, with its tender and the first box-car off the rails behind it.

Tom Thumb was in the ditch with a broken leg and Scott

A place in history

was unhurt. But Jumbo, trapped between the derailed locomotive and the circus train, was mortally injured. He had given a mighty roar just as the engine struck him, but now he lay quietly on his side and his old keeper tried to comfort him. In a few minutes, with his trunk holding onto Scott's hand, Jumbo died.

Even under ordinary circumstances a busy railway yard by night was a stimulating spectacle: a bustling, clanking island of steam, smoke, yellow fires and oil-lamps. Now, the grotesque angles of the derailed engine and trucks, the twisted rails and wreckage, and the swarms of labouring men, gave the scene a frightening urgency, touched with the fantasy of horror by the cries of animals, glimpses of the scattered paraphernalia of the circus, and the body of a huge elephant with a weeping man by its side.

Death by the railroad

Under the business-like orders of the circus loadmaster and senior railwaymen the wreckage was cleared, repairs made, and the engine set on the rails again. By next morning the line was restored to running order and the circus train had moved off to its engagement in the next town, taking Tom Thumb, whose broken leg had been set and splinted during the night by Newman and the circus veterinary assistant. Jumbo's body, released from the wreckage, was left under guard lying on the embankment.

With daylight came the sightseers, drawn in their hundreds to a small rail crash with only a single fatal casualty, but that one of such fame that the opportunity of seeing the huge body was irresistible. Some of them tried to get hold of souvenirs—a hair from the tail, a fragment of ivory, or a piece of hide. The single guard on the body was supplemented by several policemen, until someone had an idea and put up a fence which controlled the crowd and made it possible to charge five cents admission. Those spectators whose macabre tastes were particularly strong, and who had the time and stomach to remain at the scene, were treated to a surfeit of entertainment. Two of Professor Ward's assistants from the Natural Science Establishment at Rochester N.Y. arrived to claim the skin and skeleton in accordance with the plans already made by Barnum. Akeley, who was the experienced taxidermist in charge of the work, wasted little time once he got to St Thomas. He bought all the suitable preservatives from chemists in the neighbourhood, he arranged with a local meat processing factory that they would deal with the problem of separating flesh from the hide and the skeleton, and he hired a local butcher and a couple of assistants to carve up the body along the chalk lines he marked out for them. The gargantuan dissection required one man to work inside the body, a gruesome task from which he had to emerge every few minutes for fresh air, and which, he said, gave him a considerable fellow feeling with Jonah. He discovered among the contents of the elephant's stomach: 'about a peck of stones and a hatful of English pennies', gold and silver coins, a bunch of keys, a police whistle, lead seals from railway trucks, many little trinkets of metal and glass, a few screws and rivets, and pieces of wire from hay bales.[9] Many of the much travelled pennies were distributed as souvenirs among those involved in the unpleasant and difficult operation when it was successfully accomplished. The skin and skeleton were sent off to Ward's establishment at Rochester to be properly mounted, while back in St Thomas, pots of Jumbo grease, produced by the rendering down of the flesh in the factory, were hawked by cheap-jacks as a sovereign remedy for most common ailments and deficiencies.

The news of Jumbo's death was telegraphed all over the world, and obituary notices appeared in the Press in America and England, and in foreign countries which followed the activities of the two great nations. The local paper[10] in St Thomas, Ontario published its tribute in the form of a drawing of an elaborately inscribed memorial tablet headed 'In Memory of JUMBO, King of Elephants.' *The New York Times*, *The Times* of London, and *The Daily Telegraph* all published long news items and comment. One British weekly, *The Graphic*, remarked[11], 'never before, perhaps, in the world's history have so many people been affectionately interested in the fortunes of a four-footed personage whom it seems quite a libel to style a "brute beast".' *The Spectator*'s comment[12] was similar, but went on to make a serious observation on the psychology of those who despise popular enthusiasm: 'Animals, like men, have continuous destinies, and Jumbo, the great elephant, had his. It was his destiny to attract more attention than any other elephant which ever existed, and it pursued him till his death. Alone of his race he has been killed by a railway locomotive . . . . It is amusing to observe the contempt with which the "craze" about Jumbo is still spoken of. What was there contemptible about it? If one person had been interested in the huge beast nobody would have been annoyed; but because a million ones were interested, the interest was pronounced insane.' *Punch*,[13] however, perhaps epitomised the more general contemporary attitude of materialistic unconcern, treating the death of the real animal rather like, say, the sad end of a nursery teddy eaten by a goat:

Alas, poor Jumbo! Here's the fruit
Of faithless Barnum's greed of gain.
How sad that so well trained a brute
Should owe his exit to a train!

Barnum's own account of Jumbo's death on the railway was more highly coloured than the eye-witness reports. His story had Jumbo saving the life of Tom Thumb by picking him up and throwing him to safety before sacrificing his own life in a head-on charge at the approaching engine. When Barnum was interviewed after the accident he told the *New York Times* reporter that Jumbo's life was not insured:[14] 'the loss is a total one, unless the railroad company is liable, and I'm not sure that I would sue for damages in any event. Poor Scott! I don't know what he'll do without Jumbo. He cares nothing for human companionship. Jumbo was all the world to him.'

The question of responsibility for the accident was widely discussed. No blame was attached to the engine driver, who was only slightly injured in the crash (he died twenty years later in the San Francisco earthquake). The railway company claimed that the circus should have loaded their wagons at a proper crossing where there would have been a railwayman to warn of the approach of the special train. On their side, the circus declared that a railway official had given them an assurance of a clear half hour before any train was due. Barnum decided to bring a hundred thousand dollar action against the Grand Trunk Railway, but it was settled out of court, the railway company agreeing to pay a sum of five thousand dollars plus free transport for the circus in Canada on the next year's tour. The details of this tour were formally included in the settlement and—whether before or after it was drawn up—an astute railway lawyer saw that one town was omitted. When the circus came to visit this town, the railway charged an exorbitant price, five thousand dollars, for a very short journey. In spite of having been outwitted, Barnum appreciated the trickery of his opponent, in rather the same way as the public enjoyed Barnum's own trickery.

Jumbo's skin, and the bones of his skeleton, were safely received at the Natural Science Establishment in Rochester, and the task of mounting them took five months. The skin, which weighed 1500 pounds, was nearly one and a half inches thick in places, and the skeleton weighed 2400 pounds. The taxidermists made a large supporting frame of steel rods and wood on which the skin was stretched and fixed into place in natural folds and creases with over seventy thousand nails.

On 26 February 1886 Barnum gave a big reception to the Press to publicise the completion of the work on the skeleton and the stuffed skin. One odd feature of the reception gives weight to the impression that Barnum had always regarded Jumbo as a museum curio that needed feeding, rather than as a sentient creature suitable for exhibition. But this is not to say that he was unfeeling by the standards of his time: a time when public hangings, badger-baiting, and rat-killing contests in pubs were only in the recent past, and world wild-life conservation was generations ahead. A lavish meal was provided by Barnum at the reception, and some of the more important guests were given small inscribed slices of ivory from Jumbo's tusks as souvenirs.[15] One of the dishes on the menu was a jelly laced with powder made by grinding up a pound and a half of the tusks. Actually to consume the star at a celebrity luncheon was a unique concept, more extravagant even than the blackest thoughts of guests bored by an interminable speech.

While the taxidermists were working on Jumbo Barnum had brought to a conclusion the negotiations, interrupted two years before, for the purchase of Alice from the London Zoo. With Jumbo's mounted skin and skeleton, she was intended to complete a mausoleum-like trio of relics of greatness. Barnum, whose eyes would have

Zoological Society's Gardens,
Regent's Park,
London, N.W.

Augt 27th 1883

333

Dear Sir

Will you authorize me to sell Alice the female African Elephant and at what price, I have seen Mr Barnum and I think I can manage to dispose of the Elephant but I must let him know immediately the terms

Yours faithfully

A. D. Bartlett

P L Sclater Esq

gleamed if he had lived to see the shuffling queue outside the Kremlin, had long planned this exhibit, but the arrangements, which got as far as loading plans, had fallen through two years before, just at the time when the White Elephant was being lodged at Regent's Park en route for America. It is not clear whether the deal collapsed because the Zoological Council thought it imprudent to publicise further a connection with Barnum's Show, which so many of the Fellows deplored, or whether Barnum and his partners were disenchanted with elephants because the public never took to Toung Taloung as they had to Jumbo now lost to the show, at least in the living flesh. Barnum reopened negotiations, and in January 1886 he cabled Bartlett, 'Will take Alice. Have sent money. Barnum.'[16]

A place in history

Alice was removed to America without incident, although Barnum believed—or perhaps hoped—that there might be a legal move to prevent the sale. He cabled Bartlett to engage an attorney immediately, but was reassured that nothing was known in London of any repetition of the Chancery Court action which had detained Jumbo.

Alice went on the circus tour in America during 1886 with the two massive Jumbo exhibits, the whole tableau being in the charge of the melancholy Scott, now something of a curio himself.

In the course of Barnum's life, disastrous fires disrupted his affairs remarkably often.[17] In 1857 Iranistan, the great Oriental palace he built for himself in Bridgeport, was destroyed in a spectacular blaze; his American Museum, badly damaged in 1864 in the Confederate plot to burn New York as a reprisal for Atlanta, was destroyed by an accidental fire a few months later; and the new American Museum built to replace it was completely gutted in 1868. In the winter of 1886 there was a very bad fire in the circus quarters at Bridgeport and, although the stuffed Jumbo and his skeleton were saved, Alice was killed.

When Jumbo was taken away from London in 1882 Barnum had suggested that he would soon bring him back again, possibly permanently. In 1889 he did at last

Opposite: *Bartlett's request to sell Alice*

keep this half-promise—after a fashion—when Barnum and Bailey's Circus crossed the Atlantic, bringing the stuffed Jumbo and his skeleton. With them came a shipload of animals and equipment, and a multitude of performers, supplemented to the number of twelve hundred by Guardsmen engaged in London, for a season of one hundred days at Olympia—an even bigger arena than the Madison Square Garden. The trip was Bailey's idea, and the venture risked over a quarter of a million pounds, all to be recouped from the admission money. Even at Olympia, the audience could not exceed about fifteen thousand per performance, several thousand of whom might have paid only two shillings for a seat, or even one shilling on two special cheap days each week.

It had taken Bailey some time to overcome Barnum's opposition to this London season. The old man had feared that he would not be welcomed by the English people because his long and well-publicised career as a

Barnum Room at Tufts

Museum of Natural History, New York

'humbug' had culminated in his making off with the nation's most famous pet in dubious circumstances, and carelessly allowing him to meet a premature and harrowing death on the railway. But Bailey's business judgement was proved to be sound, and Barnum's surprising loss of confidence in his own life-style was unjustified. The imp is usually more attractive than the angel, and people flocked to Olympia, many of them looking upon Barnum himself as the principal exhibit.

The London papers gave very favourable reviews to the show, which followed the same pattern each day: two separate performances with a two hour interval between them, when the public could inspect the menagerie and the collection of curios and freaks. If Jumbo was the largest exhibit, then the smallest was probably eighteen-year-old Master Dudley Foster, said to be eight pounds in weight and thirty-one inches tall. *The Times* reported,[18]

> The three simultaneous circuses, together with the variety shows give way to one culminating historical spectacle in which the full strength of the *personnel* is employed—a series of tableaux called 'Nero, or the Destruction of Rome'; while by way of prelude to the grandiose operations in the arena, a large menagerie, and a host of museum curiosities, monstrosities, and other sights such as only America can produce . . . . curiosities which secured Mr Barnum his reputation in the first instance, for the great showman was a 'museum' man before he took up the circus business . . . .

The advertisements promised that Mr Barnum would be present at every performance, and he usually was. When he saw the extent of his popularity Barnum took to making a spectacular entrance, driving in an open carriage round the rings so that all could see him, and then standing up to greet the audience with 'Waal, I'm Barnum', and acknowledge the outburst of clapping and cheers. Queen

'Waal, I'm Barnum'

Victoria, the Prince of Wales, and Gladstone all honoured the circus with a visit and some expression of personal congratulation to Barnum. A testimonial banquet given for him by prominent members of the British aristocracy completed Barnum's triumph on this, his last visit to England.

A place in history

It was Jumbo's last visit too. When the circus returned to America the skeleton and the stuffed skin found permanent homes in museums. Before 1900 the great American museums had relied heavily upon circus and menagerie proprietors donating dead animals as zoological specimens. Barnum had helped many in this way, ensuring whenever possible, of course, that his name was well publicised in connection with the gift.

There had been some competition for Jumbo's skeleton between the American Museum of Natural History in New York and the Smithsonian Institute in Washington,[19] but it eventually went to New York where, the American journal *Natural History* wrote in 1952, 'Its limbs are now polished and grimy from the little hands of thousands of

Jumbo model in the British Museum of Natural History

admiring children that have fondled it during the past 62 years.' As recently as 1974 Jumbo's skeleton was the massive centre-piece of a circus exhibition put on by the Museum of Natural History, and in 1976 he moves to new quarters in a reconstructed hall in the department of mammology.

The stuffed Jumbo went to Tuft's College, Medford, Massachusetts, to which Barnum had previously made a number of generous gifts, and it became the principal feature of a special small museum containing Barnum's desk and other memorabilia. Jumbo was incorporated into the College crest, and its sports teams were often encouraged with the cry of 'Come on the Jumbos'. In death as in life, offerings of coins were made to Jumbo. The students considered that a small coin placed in his trunk helped to bring the hoped-for result in an examination. Perhaps the coins which had been offered earlier to the living Jumbo were a manifestation of this later wishing-well behaviour, supporting the idea that people pay special attention to an elephant because they have atavistic

Cast of Jumbo's upper molars

feelings that the great beast is a god to be propitiated. Sadly, the scourge of fire, which so often fell upon Barnum during his lifetime, did so again in 1975, when the building housing the Barnum museum at Tufts University was burned down and the stuffed Jumbo lost with almost everything else. The university newspaper commented[20] on the damage, which amounted to something over two million dollars, and said that compared with the loss of research equipment and results 'Jumbo's demise, to the hardhearted, may seem negligible. But to Tufts sports fans, alumni who remember when, circus lovers, and just plain sentimentalists, Monday's fire destroyed the university's embodiment of the fantasy of rah-rah College Life—a tradition.'

A place in history

A little bit of Jumbo remains still in England. In 1886 Ward's Natural Science Establishment in Rochester N.Y., where the skeleton and skin had been mounted, sent a section of one of Jumbo's tusks and a plaster cast of his upper molars to the Natural History Section of the British Museum in South Kensington. Looking at this cast, even the layman is at once struck by the fact that there is clearly something wrong with the teeth, the two sides of the jaw being grossly asymmetric. Experts confirm that there is pronounced abnormality in the teeth[21] very likely to have caused the animal permanent chronic discomfort even after the painful process of eruption was completed. There is some room for speculation that Jumbo might have needed, and been given, sedatives to ensure the passive demeanour which he always displayed in the circus ring.

Soon after his return from England after the successful season at Olympia, Barnum became seriously ill, was confined to bed for many weeks, and on 7 April 1891 he died at home in Bridgeport. Of all his obituaries, perhaps that of the New York *Evening Sun* was most apposite. It was published on 24 March, with his permission, when death seemed imminent, so that he might satisfy his curiosity to know what the world would say of him when he had gone. More conventionally posthumous, *The Times* obituary said that 'he created the *métier* of showman on a grandiose scale, worthy to be professed by a man of genius . . . . To live on, by, and before the public was his ideal . . . . His name is a proverb already, and a proverb it will continue.' Barnum would have liked that, and his wish for respectable status as well as theatrical fame would have been gratified by a serious appraisal of his contribution to the popularisation of natural history, published in the *Journal of the History of Ideas* in 1959.

Scott, who had stayed on with the circus after the death of Jumbo and then of Alice, became a rather pathetic old man. He was convinced that Barnum would leave him a generous legacy, but all he got was a copy of Barnum's autobiography.[22] Bartlett died in May 1897 and was buried in Highgate Cemetery, not far from the Zoological Gardens where his influence had done so much to shape the future style not only of the London Zoo but of others all over the world. Like Barnum, his early career was not that in which he achieved fame, although Bartlett's years as a taxidermist were not without their triumphs, perhaps the most notable being his reconstruction of the dodo from a few fragments salvaged after the authorities at Oxford had thrown away the very last specimen in the world of this extinct bird.

Today Bartlett's name is known only in specialised zoological circles, and *The Times* prediction that Barnum's name would remain a proverb seems somewhat tenuous, but Jumbo is a living, growing part of the language. His name has passed into folk-lore as the rhyming slang 'jumbo's trunk', meaning drunk,[23] and the scatter-word in a children's chasing game. The other players gather round the chaser, who recites their names in turn until, after mounting suspense, he substitutes for one of the names a shout of 'Jumbo', at which they all rush away from him and the hunt begins.[24]

The story of Jumbo was told and retold many times in American and British newspapers and magazines through the first half of the twentieth century on the occasion of anniversaries or the deaths of those connected with the affair. It was still fresh enough in November 1935 for

Billy Rose to put on a musical called *Jumbo* at the New York Hippodrome, with Paul Whiteman and Jimmy Durante, and words and music by Rodgers and Hart. More recently MGM made a film version starring Doris Day, the hit song being *The Most Beautiful Girl in the World*.

A place in history

It needed more than a single circumstance to bring about Jumbo's fame: he was the right animal, with the right name, and his adventure took place at the right time in the hands of the right publicist. The time was one of social change. The gap between the poor and the well-to-do remained wide—'Outward Bound' still meant emigration for ragged-school boys—but entertainments and amusements were being increasingly shared by all classes. The spread of newspapers promoted public interest in these fields, and Barnum was just the man to manipulate such publicity.

The wonder and affection felt by the public for all elephants was in Jumbo's case strongly reinforced by

Finale of MGM's Jumbo *with Doris Day and Jimmy Durante*

his extraordinary size and by the catchword quality of his name. The second half of Mumbo Jumbo, casually chosen, has become the synonym for elephant, much as the combination of St Peter's Field and Waterloo made Peterloo a most famous working class massacre. But among the cognominal nouns in the dictionary—sandwich, wellington, zeppelin; a generally noble list—jumbo is unique as a pet name, and one now gaining ground as an adjective.

If jumbo is a word from the nursery that has colonised the adult world and found a home in every dictionary, then Jumbo himself, as an object to be touched and wondered at, has survived from the nineteenth into the twentieth century and—in his new quarters at the American Museum of Natural History, New York—seems set to stand silent and majestic into the twenty-first.

Notes

The Noah's Ark Society

1 *Household Words* Vol. 3, p235, 1851
2 Close Rolls, January, 1255
3 *Animal Intelligence* by Romanes (Keegan Paul Trench, 1882)
4 *Wild Animals in Captivity* by A. D. Bartlett (Chapman and Hall, 1899)
5 *A History of the Earth and Animated Nature* by Oliver Goldsmith (Fullarton, 1857)
6 *Oxford English Dictionary* (1933)
7 *Wild Animals in Captivity* by A. D. Bartlett (Chapman and Hall, 1899)
8 *Ibid*
9 *Western Daily Mercury*, 15 March, 1882
10 *Animal World*, March, 1882
11 Zoological Society of London Archives

Walking in the Zoo

1 *Walking in the Zoo* by Sweny and Lee (Hopwood and Crew, 1867)
2 *Elephants* by Carrington (Chatto and Windus/Penguin, 1958)
3 *Wild Animals in Captivity* by A. D. Bartlett (Chapman and Hall, 1899)
4 *The Zoo Story* by Brightwell (Museum Press, 1952)
5 *The Spectator*, 25 February, 1882

Trouble with pachyderms

1 *Wild Animals in Captivity* by A. D. Bartlett (Chapman and Hall, 1899)
2 *Ibid*
3 *Household Words* Vol. 2, p49, 1850
4 *Ibid* Vol. 4, p156, 1851
5 *Elephants* by Carrington (Chatto and Windus/Penguin, 1958)
6 *The Natural History of the African Elephant* by Sikes (Weidenfeld and Nicolson, 1971)
7 *Ibid*
8 14 December, 1881, Zoological Society of London Archives

Rally to Jumbo's defence

1 *Saturday Review*, 25 February, 1882
2 *Echo*, 18 February, 1882
3 *Daily Telegraph*, 20 February, 1882
4 *Animal World*, 1 March, 1884
5 *Standard*, 21 February, 1882
6 *Illustrated London News*, 25 February, 1882
7 *Pall Mall Gazette*, 21 February, 1882
8 *Daily Telegraph*, 22 February, 1882
9 Zoological Society of London Archives
10 Harvard Museum of Theatre
11 *Punch*, 4 March, 1882
12 *The Spectator*, 25 February, 1882
13 *Ibid*, 4 March, 1882
14 *Saturday Review*, 25 February, 1882
15 21 February, 1882, Zoological Society of London Archives
16 *Ibid*, 16 March, 1882
17 *Daily Telegraph*, 24 February, 1882
18 *The Zoological Society of London* by Scherren (Cassell, 1905)
19 *Wild Animals in Captivity* by A. D. Bartlett (Chapman and Hall, 1899)
20 *The Fabulous Showman* by Irving Wallace (Hutchinson, 1960)
21 16 March, 1882, Zoological Society of London Archives
22 *Vanity Fair*, 25 February, 1882
23 *Morning Post*, 22 February, 1882
24 *John Ruskin* by Wilenski (Faber and Faber, 1933)
25 *New York Times*, 11 April, 1882
26 Bickersteth, 25 February, 1882, Royal Archives, Windsor Castle, P26/32
27 21 March, 1882, Zoological Society of London Archives
28 *The Times*, 6 March, 1882
29 *Ibid*, 7 March, 1882
30 Chancery Division Law Report, 8 March, 1882

Down the river

1 *Western Daily Mercury*, 13 March, 1882
2 *Animal World*, 1 March, 1884
3 *New York Herald*
4 *Animal World*, 1 March 1884
5 *Western Daily Mercury*, 29 March, 1882
6 Ross. Penny Library. Strand, London
7 *The Fabulous Showman* by Irving Wallace (Hutchinson, 1960)

8 *Vanity Fair*, 11 March, 1882
9 *Punch*, 4 March, 1882
10 *The Times*, 22 March, 1882
11 *Ibid*, 23 March, 1882
12 *Western Daily Mercury*, 24 March, 1882
13 Labouchere. *Hansard*, 10 March, 1882
14 *Solicitors Journal*, March, 1882
15 *The Times*, 27 March, 1882

Over the sea to Broadway

1 *Western Daily Mercury*, 27 March, 1882
2 *Manchester Evening News*, 28 March, 1882
3 *New York Herald*, 11 April, 1882
4 Private communication. W. Crompton, Head Keeper of Elephants, London Zoo
5 *All About Elephants* by Burger (W. H. Allen, 1966)

The Greatest Show on Earth

1 *The Fabulous Showman* by Irving Wallace (Hutchinson, 1960)
2 *Animal World*, 1 March, 1884
3 *Nation*, March, 1882
4 Routledge, 1882
5 Lydekker, *Proc. Zoo. Soc. London*, April, 1907
6 Tyrwhitt-Drake, Staffordshire Pottery Animals, *Country Life*, 9 June, 1955
7 *Early American Pressed Glass* by Ruth Webb Lee (Northboro Mass., 1946)
8 *Big Top* by Bradna and Spence (Simon and Schuster, 1952)
9 Hornaday, *Bulletin New York Zool. Soc.* No. 49, 1911
10 *Sunday News*, 26 September, 1954

A place in history

1 *Natural History*, January, 1952. 9 October, 1883
2 Bartlett, 27 August, 1883, Zoological Society of London Archives
3 *The English Governess at the Siamese Court* by Leonowens (London, 1870)
4 *The Spectator*, January, 1884
5 *Animal World*, 1 February, 1884

6 *Ibid*, 1 March, 1884
7 *The Fabulous Showman* by Irving Wallace (Hutchinson, 1960)
8 *Animal World*, 1 March, 1884
9 *Nature*, 1 October, 1885
10 *Daily Times*, 17 September, 1885
11 *The Graphic*, 17 October, 1885
12 *The Spectator*, 19 September, 1885
13 *Punch*, 26 September, 1885
14 *New York Times*, 17 September, 1885
15 *Natural History*, January, 1952
16 Zoological Society of London Archives
17 *The Fabulous Showman* by Irving Wallace (Hutchinson, 1960)
18 *The Times*, 12 November, 1889
19 Hornaby to Barnum, 24 March, 1890, Smithsonian Archives. Jessep to Barnum, 8 April, 1889, American Museum of Natural History Archives
20 Julie Salamon, *The Tufts Observer*, 18 April, 1975
21 Private communication, Dr A. W. Gentry, British Museum (Nat. Hist.) *et al.*
22 *Circus Parade* by Conklin (Harper, NY, 1921)
23 *Slang Vol. I* by Partridge (Routledge, 1961)
24 *Children's Games in Street and Playground* by Opie (Oxford UP, 1969)

Index